SACRED SUMMITS

John Muir (1838–1914)

SACRED SUMMITS

John Muir's Greatest Climbs

Edited and Introduced by
Graham White

CANONGATE

First published in Great Britain in 1999 by Canongate Books Ltd,
14 High Street, Edinburgh EH1 1TE

10 9 8 7 6 5 4 3 2 1

Introduction copyright © Graham White 1999
'John Muir and Vertical Sauntering' copyright © Arthur W Ewart 1993;
'John Muir and the Range of Light' copyright © Francis P Farquhar 1965;
'A Scottish Climber on Cathedral Peak' copyright © Ken Crocket 1999,
'John Muir's Ascent of Mount Rainer' copyright © Aubrey L Haines 1962

British Library Cataloguing-in-Publication Data
A catalogue record for this book is available on request from the British Library

ISBN 086241 785 6

Typeset by Hewer Text Ltd, Edinburgh
Printed and bound in Finland by WSOY

CONTENTS

INTRODUCTION by Graham White   xi

Timeline of Muir's Mountain Ascents   xxix

1. JOHN MUIR AND VERTICAL SAUNTERING *Arthur W Ewart*   1

2. JOHN MUIR AND THE RANGE OF LIGHT
   Francis P Farquhar   18

3. A SCOTTISH CLIMBER ON CATHEDRAL PEAK *Ken Crocket*   39

4. THE TUOLUMNE CAMP *John Muir*   51

5. A NEAR VIEW OF THE HIGH SIERRA *John Muir*   63

6. MOUNTAIN THOUGHTS *John Muir*   80

7. PRAYERS IN THE HIGHER MOUNTAIN TEMPLES – OR A
   GEOLOGIST'S WINTER WALK *John Muir*   88

8. A PERILOUS NIGHT ON SHASTA'S SUMMIT *John Muir*   95

9. THE SOUTH DOME *John Muir*   109

10. THE RESCUE ON GLENORA PEAK *Samuel Hall Young*   114

11. THE STICKEEN RIVER *John Muir*   129

12. GLENORA PEAK *John Muir*   137

13. AN ASCENT OF MOUNT RAINIER *John Muir*   144

14. JOHN MUIR'S ASCENT OF MOUNT RAINIER
    Aubrey L Haines   150

Bibliography   161

PREFACE

The volume was inspired by Richard Fleck's collection of John Muir's climbing adventures, first published as *John Muir, Mountaineering Essays* in 1989. In this book Fleck selected many of Muir's classic mountaineering accounts, but unfortunately the collection is little known in the UK. In 1997 I proposed a Scottish edition of Fleck's book to try and bring it to a wider audience, but for various publishing reasons this proved impractical.

Fortunately Canongate Books later agreed to support a wider compilation, including commentaries by academics and climbers on Muir's mountain achievements, which resulted in the present volume. I have gratefully built upon Richard Fleck's selections from Muir but have included other contributions from Arthur W Ewart, Francis Farquhar, Aubrey L Haines, Ken Crocket, and Muir's contemporary Samuel Hall Young.

Hopefully this will be of equal value in bringing Muir to a wider audience of climbers and conservationists in both America and the UK.

ACKNOWLEDGEMENTS

The editor would like to thank Judy and Neville Moir at Canongate, as well as the following individuals and agencies for their help in creating this book.

Professor Richard Fleck, for his original compilation of *John Muir: Mountaineering Essays*.

Professor Ronald Limbaugh at the John Muir Centre for Regional Studies, University of the Pacific for his advice on John Muir and the history of the conservation movement in the USA.

Judge Philip Berry, Legal Adviser to the Sierra Club for his personal survey of Muir's historic climbs in the American climbing literature on my behalf.

Ron Eber, Muir scholar, for his editorial advice and academic contacts in the United States.

Sally Miller and University of New Mexico Press for permission to publish Arthur W Ewart's *Vertical Sauntering* from *John Muir, Life and Work*.

The Sierra Club and University of California Press for permission to publish Francis P Farquhar's *John Muir and the Range of Light* from *History of the Sierra Nevada*.

Aubrey L Haines and Oregon Historical Society for permission to publish *John Muir's Ascent of Mt Rainier*, from *Mountain Fever – Historic Conquests of Rainier*.

Ken Crocket of the Scottish Mountaineering Club for his original essay, *A Scottish Climber's View of Cathedral Peak*, and for his photographs of this area.

Dr Terry Isles and Nigel Hawkins, of the John Muir Trust, for their photographs of the High Sierra.

Graham White
Dunbar, Scotland
March 1999

INTRODUCTION

This book offers various perspectives on John Muir's mountaineering achievements, using his own writings and commentaries by academics, historians and climbers. These illuminate the development of Muir's mountain philosophy and his conservation ethos, in which many would judge that he was a century ahead of his time. But why should the modern mountaineer, rock-climber or hill-walker, be remotely interested in the words and achievements of a Victorian who enjoyed his best climbing more than a century ago? In fact, Muir's ideas about climbing and conservation are acutely relevant to our own era, since the environmental crises which he faced were driven by exactly the same forces of greed and exploitation as those which confront us today. Muir's approach to mountaineering was nature-centred rather than human-centred and the 'quality' of the experience was more important than the 'quantity'. Muir was interested in the whole experience: the canyon's depths, or the alpine meadows, were just as inviting as the mountain peak. Every rock, every plant and animal encountered on each step of the whole journey was to be studied and experienced to the full: with mind and body, intellect and emotion, spirit and soul. For Muir, the highest peak attained was only the mid-point and climax of a circular pilgrimage, rather than the terminus of a summit assault.

This distinction between the 'quantitative' and the 'qualitative' aspects of the mountain experience is difficult to put into words, and my only recourse is to a personal tale. The beginnings of my own insight came in 1980 – I had just returned from following the John Muir Trail over a hundred miles through the High Sierra at an average altitude of 10,000 feet, and I was still haunted by the experience. Back in the UK, I was invited to accompany a party of outdoor-pursuit instructors on a trip to the Italian Dolomites. On the first day we climbed a 3000 metre peak, using the *via ferrata* system of iron ladders and steel cables, scaling airy precipices which were otherwise far beyond my scrambling ability.

The Dolomites are ancient coral reefs whose limestone terraces were thrust up over 10,000 feet in former geological epochs and their calciferous soils foster an explosion of plants and wildlife. The alpine slopes were dotted with purple gentians, pink and white saxifrage, and Lady's Slipper orchids. In the higher gullies, chamois perched on featureless rock walls, their razor hooves finding purchase where we would need pitons. On the cliffs, alpine choughs stalled and tumbled in the breeze, their scarlet beaks sharp against the blue, while Mediterranean swifts scythed the rocky battlements.

It was hard keeping pace with the professionals, who competed in climbing as fast as possible; conversation was minimal and rivalry was rampant. Reaching the summit at noon, we had lunched for perhaps fifteen minutes when our leader abruptly announced that we should 'get going' on the descent. I was non-plussed. We could not climb another peak that day; there were eight hours of daylight left, and we had no plans for the afternoon. Why could we not just stay here for an hour or two? The leader's reaction was one of genuine puzzlement; why would you want to stay longer? What was there 'to do' here? And besides, we had already 'done' this mountain – i.e., we had ticked it off in the guidebook of alpine climbs. He also joked that I must be a little 'odd' to want to remain here; just what was the point? It was my turn to be baffled; surely, 'the point' of lingering in this alpine paradise was self-evident. We basked in hot sunshine, stunning views of snow-capped mountains presented themselves on every side, while above us the azure void faded imperceptibly to the indigo of space. However, I was very much the invited guest; the group consensus was clear, and we set off down the mountain. The descent was even more competitive than the climb – the teachers seemed desperate to cover the ground as quickly as possible; at times we almost ran, as if harried by some unknown pursuer. There was no time to pause and savour the landscape, plants, birds or animals. Ecology was evidently for wimps.

Much later, on reflection, I realised that this climb was a good example of the goal-oriented, 'quantitative' ethos prevalent in outdoor pursuits at that time. Environmental education was little known in Scotland, and outdoor-education teachers saw themselves as simply conveying a set of technical skills in climbing, canoeing and skiing. The criteria of a 'successful' climb thus became almost purely quantitative: How high did you climb? How quickly did you climb and how fast did you descend? How hard were the pitches? What equipment was used? How many peaks did you conquer? And, above all, who came first? This fosters a competitive approach to peak-bagging that has much in common with train-spotting or stamp-collecting. Muir's mountain ethos, made clear in the following abstracts, is radically different from the goal-oriented, tick-list and number-obsessed attitude which, even today, often prevails. He wrote:

> This was my 'method of study': I drifted about from rock to rock, from stream to stream. Where night found me, there I camped. When I discovered a new plant, I sat down beside it, for a minute or a day, to make its acquaintance and try to hear what it had to say. When I came to moraines or ice-scratches upon the rocks, I traced them, learning what I could of the glaciers that made them. I asked the boulders I met whence they came and whither they were going. I followed to their fountains the various soils upon which the forests and meadows are planted; and when I discovered a mountain or rock of marked form or structure, I climbed about it, comparing it with its neighbours, marking its relation to the forces that had acted upon it, glaciers, streams, avalanches, etc., in seeking to account for its form, finish, position and general character.[1]

Muir immersed himself in the whole experience, rather than mechanically notching-up another spot-height and recording the fact that he had 'conquered' another peak. His object was to explore, study and enjoy the entire mountain: its rocks, canyons, glaciers, rivers, plants and animals, as well as the myriad connections which constitute an ecosystem.

For Muir, mountaineering was definitely an extreme physical challenge; but it was also an ecological, aesthetic and spiritual journey of discovery. An approach which educators and the mountaineering community must surely take to heart if any vestige of undamaged wilderness is to survive the coming century.

John Muir, born 21st April 1838 in Dunbar, Scotland, is known throughout the USA as the 'Father of the American National Parks', a popular title which honours his seminal role in the national conservation movement. American academics draw a clear distinction between Muir's 'preservationist' ethos and that of 'conservationists' like President Teddy Roosevelt and Gifford Pinchot – the first head of America's Forest Service. They stress that Muir was a 'preservationist', who wanted to preserve areas of pristine wilderness, untouched for all time. In contrast, Roosevelt and Pinchot were utilitarian 'conservationists', who regarded Nature as largely existing for human benefit; natural resources were to be 'wisely used' so as to benefit the greatest number of people, for the greatest length of time. But of course, there is no hard, or clear-cut distinction, between these two positions. Muir certainly wanted to preserve areas of wilderness, unmarked by human development, since he had experienced the profound scientific, aesthetic and spiritual value of such places.

But he was also a pragmatist, and a working farmer, who knew that only a part of the wilderness could be protected in national parks, and inevitably, most land would be surrendered to agricultural and industrial development. It is often forgotten that Muir voted for cars to be allowed into Yosemite Valley in 1906; partly because he knew that the car lobby could not be resisted, but also because he felt that the struggle to conserve wilderness could only be won if millions of people had access to it, via the car and the railroad.

In the UK, where we have no untouched wilderness at all, in the American sense, such distinctions can seem rather academic to most conservationists. But the difference becomes clear if one spends a day in Yosemite Valley (with its supermarket, interpretation centres, launderettes, art galleries, car parks and pizzerias), followed by a week in the 1500 square miles of unspoiled wilderness in the wider Yosemite National Park. Whatever the label we ascribe to him, it is clear that from the 1870s until his death in 1914, Muir campaigned tirelessly for the protection of wilderness and wildlife, in articles which kept the issue high on the national agenda. As founding

Introduction

President of the Sierra Club in 1892, he attracted passionate and influential talents to the defence of the American environment, and together they forged a new alliance in society, which we now term 'The Conservation Movement'. Robert Underwood Johnson, his friend, publisher and political adviser, summed-up Muir's place in American history thus:

Muir's public services were not merely scientific and literary. His countrymen owe him gratitude as the pioneer of our system of national parks. Out of the fight, which he led, for the better care of the Yosemite by the State of California, grew the demand for the extension of the system. To this many persons and organisations contributed, but Muir's writings and enthusiasm were the chief forces that inspired the movement. All the other torches were lighted from his.[2]

President Theodore Roosevelt, uniquely placed to gauge the social and political tides of the 19th century, stressed that Muir was not just a dreamer; his achievements were practical and enduring:

. . . he was also what few nature-lovers are, a man able to influence contemporary thought and action on the subjects to which he had devoted his life. He was a great factor in influencing the thought of California and the thought of the entire country so as to secure the preservation of those great natural phenomena – wonderful canyons, giant trees, slopes of flower-spangled hillsides . . . our generation owes much to John Muir.[3]

The scale of the environmental legacy which Muir and the Sierra Club have bequeathed to us is evident in America's National Parks, National Monuments and National Historic Sites: 376 protected areas stretching from Hawaii to Florida and Arizona to Alaska. More than 80 million acres of wild land are conserved within the 54 national parks, and one preserve alone, the Wrangell–St Elias National Park, extends to over 13 million acres. The Forest Service, in the creation of whose earliest reserves Muir played a significant role, is responsible for 191 million acres, while the Fish and Wildlife Service manages a further 91 million acres of wild land. Consequently, over

360 million acres of American eco-systems and wildlife are protected as a result of the national movement for which John Muir carried the banner. It is hardly surprising that many Americans feel deeply indebted to Muir, nor that he has become the *Genius Loci* for the environment, particularly in California and the western states.

But there is another dimension to Muir's life, which is often overshadowed by his conservation success, namely his climbing achievements and the evolution of his conservation ethos which sprang directly from his mountain experiences. Arthur Ewart, whose essay 'John Muir and Vertical Sauntering' forms the first chapter of this compilation, declares:

> In the last quarter of the nineteenth century, John Muir was the best mountaineer in the United States. He set physical standards in the sport that are difficult to match today, and his mountaineering ethics have come to be appreciated and emulated only recently within the American climbing community.[4]

Ewart rests his judgement on the authority of Steve Roper, the noted American climber and author of the classic *Climber's Guide to the High Sierra*, who wrote:

> . . . While in Tuolumne Meadows in 1869, he [Muir] made the first ascent of the sharp and beautiful Cathedral Peak; this involved some difficult climbing of a nature not yet seen in this country. Although his mountaineering exploits are not as well known as his later geological theories, descriptive writings and long struggles to exclude sheep and lumbermen from his beloved mountains, Muir's solo ascents of Mount Ritter, Mount Whitney, and many other peaks (mentioned only obliquely in his writings) place him among the first rank of early American mountaineers.[5]

Francis Farquhar, the definitive historian of the High Sierra, whose essay 'John Muir and the Range of Light' forms Chapter Two of this book, is emphatic concerning Muir's first ascent of the east face of Mount Whitney:

Should someone of the present generation of mountain climbers feel inclined to make light of Muir's exploits, let him endeavour to duplicate it [this climb] – starting from Independence . . . on foot, with or without sleeping bag and the present-day advantage of concentrated foods, Muir had neither.[6]

It is clear that from 1869 onwards Muir intuitively deduced and developed the basic skills of solo-mountaineering and rock-climbing, without training or assistance from others. Ken Crocket, a well-known Scots climber, describes his reprise of Muir's ascent of Cathedral Peak in Chapter Three. If Muir really did climb this route to the very summit, as he is credited, then he was courageous to the point of recklessness, as can be gauged from Ken's record of his own challenging climb. Similarly, on his first ascents of Mount Ritter and the east face of Mount Whitney, Muir ventured into remote territory, from which there was no earthly hope of rescue if he should break an ankle or leg. Moreover, on his three ascents of Mount Shasta he pushed his own limits on snow and ice close to what had been attempted at that time in America.

Muir emigrated from Scotland in February 1849, but we know that long before his eleventh birthday he had acquired a taste for rocky adventures, scrambling on the volcanic cliffs of Dunbar and the crumbling walls of its thousand-year-old castle. Following his arrival in Wisconsin, he endured ten years' drudgery as unpaid 'ploughboy, well-digger and lumberjack' on the family homesteads at Fountain Lake Farm and Hickory Hill, while his father read the Bible and directed operations from a distance. This hard-bitten adolescence left Muir little time for leisure and, as far as we know, mountain climbing was not on his agenda at that time. It was not until he reached Yosemite Valley in 1869, aged thirty-one, that he became a passionate, self-taught mountaineer, eager to explore the vast wilderness of the High Sierra.

As a youth in Wisconsin, Muir acquired two heroes: Friedrich von Humboldt (1769–1859), the historic explorer of South America and central Asia; and Henry David Thoreau (1817–62), the New England philosopher who made transcendental Nature his province. Muir was unable to follow Humboldt's path until he was thirty, when he began a decade of exploration in the Sierra Nevada. His *Studies in the Sierra* broke new ground in the fields of geology, glaciology and botany; he was the first to discover living glaciers in the High Sierra and to deduce their role in sculpting the great valleys and watersheds of Yosemite. Moreover, he was first to map the distributions of the Coastal Redwood (*Sequoia sempervirens*) and the Giant Redwood (*Sequoia gigantea*) over their vast ranges. But beyond the discovery of new plant species and his radical theories of geology, Muir accomplished something of far greater importance. He began to describe a revolutionary scientific and philosophical synthesis: a unitary vision of the biosphere in which solar energy, planetary weather systems, oceans, mountain ranges, rivers, rocks, micro-organisms, plants, animals and human beings were perceived as one vast, interconnected, evolutionary flow of energy and matter. In exploring the foundations of the science which we now term 'ecology', Muir was sketching out the boundaries of a new scientific paradigm with which we are coming to terms only a century later. James Lovelock's famous Gaia Hypothesis of a self-regulating biosphere seems to have much in common with John Muir's vision of an evolving creation.

During his years of solitary climbing and exploration, Muir confided to Jeanne Carr that although he could not yet clearly descry his purpose in the new world which he was scouting, he was confident that his apparently 'pathless' road would lead him to a meaningful destiny. The path which he took, and the trail which he blazed for all to follow, we now recognise as 'Conservation'. His literary preaching of the ethical, aesthetic and scientific principles for this new perspective ushered in a new field of human awareness, which Thoreau and Emerson had first envisaged. But it should not be forgotten that, at the time, most observers thought Muir quite deranged in pursuing this life of solitary exploration; and to the frontier mentality, the idea of conservation was often anathema.

The characteristics of Muir's mountaineering style emerge from his own accounts published here, and from witnesses like Samuel Hall Young (see Chapter Ten). They include:

Climbing as a solitary activity

A clean-climbing/ minimalist use of ropes and equipment

A preference for the extended adventure and long walk-in
An extreme test of strength, skills and endurance
A refusal to ever 'turn back' from a mountain challenge
An ascetic disregard for the comforts of food, shelter and clothing
A holistic/ ecological approach to exploring 'the whole mountain'
A profound respect for all forms of life
A search for spiritual transcendence in the mountains

On the first point, Muir invariably climbed alone; he did not normally accept responsibility for other people's lives on perilous ascents. On two memorable occasions when he broke this rule, he ended up risking his life in order to rescue a companion.

The first crisis occurred during his ascent of Mount Shasta with Jerome Fay, when they were trapped by a violent electrical storm near the summit of the 14,000-foot volcano. This episode is graphically portrayed in Muir's own words in Chapter Eight, 'A Perilous Night on Shasta's Summit'. On a second occasion, Muir allowed Samuel Hall Young to accompany him on the ascent of Glenora, an 8000-foot peak in Alaska; Young came to grief near the summit in a fall which paralysed him. Having tried to leap a small gully he fell, violently dislocating both shoulders, and was left paralysed, with his legs projecting from a rock-chute, 1000 feet above the glacier.

Muir's heroic rescue of his friend, and the agony of the twelve-hour descent which ensued, are described here in his own account as well as that of Samuel Hall Young (chapters Ten and Eleven.) But there was another, more profound, reason why Muir preferred to climb alone; he exulted in the mental and spiritual freedom of solitude among the mountains. To shake the dust of the town from his feet, to be alone in the wilderness, with the mind unsullied by the chatter of companions, was the very essence of mountaineering for Muir. More than this, it was his greatest fulfilment and his personal religion: 'Christianity and Mountainanity are streams which flow from the same source'. The spiritual aspect of Muir's mountain ethos infuses all the following texts, but for a deeper exploration and analysis, one should read Richard Cartwright Austin's fine book, *Baptised into Wilderness.*[7]

Like most climbers Muir loved to pit his intelligence and climbing skills against every challenge that mountain, rock and ice could throw at him. Henry Fairfield Osborne, a close friend, wrote that whenever the topic of climbing or expeditions arose, Muir would solemnly intone: 'I never turn back' , an attitude that will resonate with many climbers.

But it is equally clear that in the boldness of all Muir's solitary ascents, it was not the mountain which was conquered, but the limitations of the self which were transcended. Muir's climbs often involved an approach of several days, through remote canyons and across unmapped ranges. Together with the climb itself, and the retreat to base camp, these expeditions could sometimes last more than a week, at altitudes above 10,000 feet. Despite this, Muir often behaved as if he were just out for a stroll. His equipment was minimal: generally the clothes he stood up in, plus a compass, thermometer and pocket barometer. He rarely took even a jacket on summit attempts and lacked all the modern paraphernalia of tent, sleeping bag, stove, waterproof clothing or specialised boots. Water was gulped from mountain freshet or glacial lake. At night he would creep beneath a juniper thicket or make a fire of resinous pine roots if frost threatened.

Challenging himself to survive in the wilderness like biblical hermits, he sought personal transcendence in communion with God and Nature. He evidently pictured himself as a latter-day John the Baptist, subsisting on 'locusts and honey'; though in Muir's case it was a less romantic hard-tack and cold tea. His rugged constitution is well documented; tall, rangy and slim, with muscles of whip-cord, he seems to have possessed an inner grit which made him impervious to the hunger and exhaustion which afflict ordinary mortals. On 8th October, 1872 he wrote to Jeanne Carr: 'I got down last night and boo! was I not weary . . . have climbed more than 24,000 feet in these ten days! – three times to the top of the glacieret of Mount Hoffman and once to mounts Lyell and McClure.'[8]

His indifference to comfort verged on a Spartan stoicism; he rarely mentions the Sierra mosquitoes, which before the advent of modern repellents must have plagued him on many nights. And though he was often a gourmet at home, he strapped himself to iron rations on his expeditions. In the back-country, where rivers teemed with trout and the forests with deer, he had only to stretch out his hand to eat like a king. Mountain-men and native Americans lived off the land; they fished the rivers, snared rabbits and roasted acorns and piñon nuts, while a rifle provided both venison and protection against grizzlies. But Muir had a profound aversion to the taking of life and would not hunt or fish for his dinner, though he did not refuse meat from others. When alone he usually carried only a bag of flour, or brick-hard loaves of bread; together with 'a screw of tea' these meagre provisions sustained him on extended journeys of several weeks and on climbs high above the tree line.

We will never know just how many mountains John Muir actually climbed, or how many first ascents he made, since he did not always bother to record them. And for Muir, the idea that one could ever 'conquer' a mountain was mere arrogance; carving one's name on a rock, or leaving a card in a summit capsule were childish grasps at a fatuous immortality. Muir had long gazed into the bottomless abyss of geological time, from which mountains had been lifted to the heights, only to be shattered, eroded and erased, by frost, rain and ice. He had traced the paths of vanished glaciers, which had ground entire ranges of adamantine granite to mere dust. Steeped in the Bible from childhood, he knew full well that 'all flesh is grass' and that in comparison with the record of the rocks, a human life was as transient as a bubble, evanescent as a mayfly. Muir concluded: 'I never left my name on any mountain, rock or tree in any wilderness I have explored or passed through, though I have spent years in the Sierra alone'.[9]

On this point, it is important to note that Muir did not complete his first book, *The Mountains of California*, until he was fifty-six years old, and only published four other volumes before his death in 1914. Almost all his important climbs were completed long before, during his thirties and forties, and it is clear that he did not seek fame through trumpeting his climbing exploits. Indeed it was largely after his death that the story of his mountain adventures came to a wider public. Most of his books were posthumous; compiled and edited from his journals by William Frederic Badè, his literary executor.

Sadly, Muir's intended book on mountaineering was never completed; the unfinished notes and fragments of this survive among the John Muir Papers at the University of the Pacific in Stockton.

The last year of the millennium is an apt moment to reconsider Muir's stature in the mountain pantheon, since it marks the 150th anniversary of his emigration to the United States. Moreover, the threats to the mountain environment, which Muir first noticed in the 1870s, are becoming increasingly urgent on every continent. Mountain habitats are among the most fragile and vulnerable parts of the biosphere; their ecosystems are particularly susceptible to damage from ozone depletion, global warming, atmospheric pollution and acid rain. Since they are usually remote from population centres, they are often the last areas to be deforested for grazing or human settlement. But they now face additional pressures, not just from the poor and the hungry, but from the global effects of tourism.

The impact of domestic tourism and climbing on Scotland's mountains has grown dramatically over the last thirty years, as it has also done in the USA. Attempts are under way to quantify visitor numbers and environmental impact, but we are probably a decade behind the American experience in devising an adequate methodology. Ken Crocket, who wrote Chapter Three of this volume, recently surveyed walkers on the tourist path up Ben Nevis. In each of two hourly samples, he counted 1500 tourists plodding to the summit of Scotland's highest mountain. This amounts to a person every two seconds, and equates more to a shopping queue than a mountain experience. The same area is also suffering environmental stress in other ways. The Scottish Mountaineering Club's web-site notes that, for some years, the environs of the Charles Inglis Clark Memorial Hut on Ben Nevis have been grossly contaminated with human sewage, revealed when the snow melts each spring. Rivers in the area already show evidence of E Coli bacteria. Sadly, the likely development of such pollution trends is the invasion of Scotland's rivers and lochs by giardia, a highly infectious parasite which causes severe dysentery. This micro-organism has spread throughout New Zealand and the whole of North America in less than a decade; all it takes is one infected mountaineer for the disease to be imported to the UK. Tragically, it is now too dangerous to drink from the wild Sierra streams where John Muir quenched his thirst, unless the water is boiled or chemically sterilised. It seems only a matter of time until the same parasite becomes established in Scotland and, once established, it will be here for eternity. Climbers will never again be able to drink from a Scottish burn or loch. Moreover, since all our household drinking water flows from the same source, this raises grave health concerns. Remarkably, there is as yet no national discussion or strategy for dealing with this threat to the mountain habitat of Scotland.

Visitor pressure has also desecrated mountains like Schiehallion – 'The Hill of the Fairies', possibly the most beautifully named of all Scotland's peaks. This used to be a relatively remote spot, bereft of all facilities, and climbers approached the mountain on foot from many points of the compass. But some years ago the Forestry Commission built a large parking-lot at the base of the mountain, complete with flush toilets, litter bins and picnic benches. The resulting visitor impact is plain for all to see; a mile-long trough gouged out of the peat, stretching from the car park to the mountain. In places this eroded gully is three-feet deep and five yards wide; in wet weather it turns into a porridge of liquid peat, immuring climbers in a true 'slough of despond'.

The second reason why Muir's climbing and conservation ethos is acutely topical relates to the larger issue of the purpose and 'mission' of national parks, in both America and the UK. A historic conflict of missions has always been apparent within the American national parks, where the preservation of wild places and wildlife has often been compromised by the over-development of commercial facilities. The developers argue that motels, galleries and restaurants are required to serve the needs of visitors, but it is also undeniable that they are the source of huge profits for the private companies who acquire the commercial contracts, or 'concessions', for the parks.

And once a profit-making company is in charge of national park visitor facilities, it will logically make every effort to attract the largest possible number of visitors in order to maximise profit. During 1996, the eight square miles of Yosemite Valley received a staggering 4 million visitors; most arrived by car, and a survey found that only a fraction ever strayed more than fifty yards from their vehicle. For many Yosemite visitors, the national park experience consists of driving from one viewpoint to the next while pausing at visitor centres, motels, restaurants, gift shops, supermarkets and galleries. In 1997 a massive flood damaged or swept away many of the buildings in the valley and conservationists hoped that the National Park

Service would grasp the opportunity to restore much of the valley to nature.

However, the current 'sustainable development-plan' intends to use the bulk of federal flood damage grants to rebuild and relocate the existing 280 motel rooms in the valley, to widen the entrance roads for cars, and encroach on natural habitats even further by building more employee housing. At the time of writing, the Sierra Club has lodged a legal complaint against the National Park Service for allegedly planning to violate the 'Wild and Scenic Rivers Act' by dumping hundreds of tons of concrete into the Merced River as foundations for a wider approach road. John Muir would weep to see the 'improvements' being planned for the national park he struggled so hard to protect.

The conflict of interest between conserving wild habitats and wildlife in Yosemite, and commercial developments to serve 'visitor needs', is evident in other American national parks. In 1888, John Muir made what was probably the sixth recorded ascent of Mount Rainier described in chapters 13 and 14 of this book. When viewed from almost any part of Seattle, Rainier's vast snow-cone is an awesome and daunting prospect for any climber. In the modern era, over two million people visit Rainier National Park annually; more than 10,000 attempt the summit and about 4500 reach the top. Such huge numbers venturing into this fragile alpine environment presents the National Park Service with some very difficult management problems; at these altitudes, where plants grow very slowly, and recover even more slowly, it is almost impossible to avoid damaging ground vegetation when visiting the area. But the major tourism issue on Rainier, apart from habitat restoration, is the abstraction of the many 55-gallon drums of sewage which accumulate at Camp Muir (10,100 feet) during the climbing season. These can only be removed by helicopter, which is expensive, noisy and potentially dangerous; but above this point, the only method of disposing of human wastes is to dig a hole in the snow adjoining the summit trail. With 10,000 people following the same narrow path each year, the pollution issue becomes serious. Americans are in danger of 'loving these places to death' as Greg Adair, a Sierra Club campaigner, recently put it.

Introduction

The history of America's national parks offers important lessons for Scotland, since the resurrected Scottish Parliament is likely to designate the country's first national parks, at Loch Lomond and Cairngorm, probably during 1999. But even before the ink has dried on the map which defines the boundaries of the Cairngorm National Park, our national conservation agency, Scottish Natural Heritage, has acceded to a private company's proposals to construct a multi-million pound funicular railway leading to a huge visitor complex on the summit of Cairngorm. Like Mount Rainier, this is one of the most fragile and vulnerable arctic-alpine habitats in Scotland, where even the simple act of walking across the summit plateau leaves traces which are still evident even a year later. A hard-fought judicial review brought by leading conservation groups against the developers was recently lost, and sadly, the development seems likely to proceed. If this private company is allowed to appropriate £9 million of the UK taxpayers' money to construct a huge industrial artefact on the slopes of Cairngorm, then we have learned nothing from the American experience.

Ecologists predict that the wildlife habitat and scenic quality of this unique mountain will be damaged for decades to come, even before it is established as a national park. This is truly a post-Orwellian world, where wildlife protection bodies prostrate themselves before the forces of economic development.

In the light of this case, conservationists now have little hope that the designation of national parks in Scotland will actually protect the wild landscapes that they are ostensibly meant to conserve. Indeed they fear that even larger amounts of taxpayers' money will flow towards the local authorities and economic development agencies, who will dominate the boards of the new parks. It is certain that this will trigger increased development of villages, towns and roads in the Highlands, all of course, in the name of 'sustainable development'. But the question remains: if the government's natural heritage agency is unable to resist a massive development at a site like Cairngorm, which is of unquestioned international environmental significance, then what chance is there for dozens of other less remarkable nature reserves in Scotland? And if the National Park Service at Yosemite, and SNH at Cairngorm, are incapable of defending the wildlife and habitats of these unique sites in the face of strong commercial and political pressures, then surely we need to redefine their primary mission?

In Scotland, the sports of mountaineering and skiing are barely a hundred years old, while Americans have perhaps thirty years additional history. For most of that time the dominant ethos has been the quantitative and competitive pursuit of record heights, new routes, fastest times and first ascents. While climbing, hill-walking and skiing were minority sports, their environmental impact was limited, but over the last thirty years the number of participants has grown exponentially. We now have a mountain-tourism industry, massive in scale and global in impact, which has triggered a new wave of economic development in peripheral mountain areas. If we are to sustain the world's fragile mountain environments through another century of recreation and tourism development, the challenge is for the climbing and hill-walking community to emulate John Muir's example by adopting a far deeper ecological ethos. Climbers in the next millennium will have to be as deeply committed to the moral and political struggle for conservation as they are to the personal and technical challenges of climbing.

The degradation of mountain environments in America was apparent to Muir as long ago as 1875 when he wrote: 'I often wonder what man will do with the mountains? Will he cut down all the trees to make ships and houses? If so, what will be the final and far upshot? Will a better civilisation come? And what then is coming? What is the human part of the mountain's destiny?'[10]

In seeking to answer that question, he was forced, much against his will, to take a leading role in the national struggle for conservation. As a result, he devoted forty years of his life to writing, campaigning and fighting to preserve the American wilderness, where he had experienced mountain triumph, scientific discovery and spiritual illumination. But even so, it took almost thirty years of writing, lobbying and fighting to return Yosemite National Park to federal protection in 1905; and even then, it did not have 'absolute' protection. For almost immediately, commercial interests sought ways to side-step the protective legislation; Muir was soon embroiled in a battle over their proposals to build a giant reservoir in Hetch Hetchy canyon, which many had naïvely assumed was protected by its national park status. He wrote at the time, in words equally relevant to today:

> In these ravaging, money mad days, monopolising San Francisco capitalists are now doing their best to destroy Yosemite Park, the greatest of all our mountain national parks . . . these devotees of ravaging commercialism seem to have a perfect contempt for Nature, and instead of lifting their eyes to the God of the mountains, lift them to the almighty dollar.[11]

Sadly, in 1913, Muir and the Sierra Club lost the battle for Hetch Hetchy; construction gangs invaded the national park, a million tons of concrete were poured, and the valley was drowned as a municipal water supply for San Francisco. Muir died of pneumonia on Christmas Eve 1914, exhausted and depressed by five years of legal and political struggle; he may well have thought that his life's work had all been in vain. But while this single battle was lost, it created a landmark for the American legal system, as the first environmental dispute to affect the national consciousness. Hundreds of similar cases have since been fought in America's courts; indeed, Muir's cohorts in the Sierra Club spend almost $80 million annually, defending the American environment. The protagonists are often the same as they were in Muir's day: the conservation bodies defending the wild places against the ambitious schemes of the federal government, the State government or the agricultural and industrial developers. Muir displayed an air of resignation when he wrote: 'The battle we have fought, and are still fighting . . . is a part of the eternal conflict between right and wrong, and we cannot expect to see the end of it.'[12]

John Muir's days of mountain glory and the conservation imperative which evolved from them are not just matters of academic or historical interest in the United States; on the contrary they are the intellectual, ethical and emotional power at the heart of the American conservation movement. It is not uncommon, in Sierra Club meetings, or in the courtrooms of America, for John Muir's spirit to be invoked in support of a point of debate.

His writings may display a Victorian sentiment at odds with the literary fashions of our day; they are perhaps at times, too passionate, too child-like and spiritually direct for our taste. But the intellectual power and ethical conviction which runs through them, sharp and shining, still cuts to the heart of today's environmental issues, as it did a century ago.

It would indeed be historic if, in time for the millennium, Muir's mountain ethos could be reclaimed for the land of his birth, to influence the creation of her first national parks.

Graham White
Dunbar, Scotland
November 1998

NOTES AND REFERENCES
1. *John of the Mountains: the Unpublished Journals of John Muir*, ed. Linnie Marsh Wolfe (1938, reprinted Madison, Univ. of Wisconsin Press, 1979) p. 69.
2. *Sierra Club Bulletin*, John Muir Memorial Issue, vol. 10, No. 1, January, 1916.
3. *The Outlook*, 6 January, 1915, pp. 27–28.
4. Arthur W Ewart, 'John Muir and Vertical Sauntering' – from: *John Muir, Life and Work*, ed. Sally Miller, (11) University of New Mexico 1993.
5. Steve Roper, *The Climber's Guide to the High Sierra* (Sierra Club Books, San Francisco, 1976), p. 13.
6. Francis P Farquhar, *History of the Sierra Nevada*, (Berkeley, University of California Press, 1966) p. 177.
7. Richard Cartwright Austin, *Baptized into Wilderness, A Christian Perspective on John Muir* (Creekside Press, Abingdon, Virginia 1989).
8. Muir, letter to Jeanne Carr: *The Life and Letters of John Muir* by William Frederic Badè (2 vols, Houghton Mifflin, Boston 1924).
9. Quote from Muir in *Mt Whitney Club Journal*, 1903.
10. Wolfe, *John of the Mountains*, p. 215.
11. 'The Hetch Hetchy Valley', *Sierra Club Bulletin*, January 1908, p. 211, 220.
12. *Sierra Club Bulletin*, January 1896, p. 276.

TIMELINE OF MUIR'S MOUNTAIN ASCENTS

1868		Muir spends his first ten days in Yosemite – a brief summer visit
1869	27th June	Climbed Sentinel Dome
	26th July	'Ramble to the summit of Mt Hoffman, eleven thousand feet high, the highest point in life's journey that my feet have yet touched.' (Actually 10,850ft)
	1st September	Climbed Mt Dana (13,053ft)
	7th September	Muir's first ascent of Cathedral Peak (10,940ft)
	8th September	'Day of climbing, scrambling, sliding on the peaks around the highest source of the Tuolumne and Merced. Climbed three of the most commanding of the mountains, whose names I don't know.'
1871	21st August	Climbed Mt McClure (12,960ft)
	7th October	Climbed Mt Clark (11,522ft) – formerly called 'The Obelisk'
	8th October	Climbed Red Peak (11,699ft)
	? October	Appears to have climbed Mt Lyell, from later correspondence. Probably this was the second ascent of the mountain; first ascent was 21st August 1871 by John Boies Tileston
1872	October	Made the first ascent of Mt Ritter (13,157ft). Extended climbs of Mt Hoffman, Lyell and McClure: '24,000 feet of climbing in ten days'. Climbed Mt Lyell (possibly for second time, according to Farquhar)
	11th December	Wrote a letter to Jeanne Carr about his first climb of Mt Lyell (13,114ft) 'the previous October'
1873	17th August	Reached 10,700ft in the Minarets. Climbed one pass of the Minarets at 11,600ft
	23rd August	Climbed Mt Davis (12,311ft). Climbed Rodgers Peak (12,978ft), called 'The Matterhorn' by Muir

	27th September	(?) Climbed Mt Humphreys on Kings River excursion or more probably Mt Darwin (13,380ft) (according to Farquhar)
	28th September	Climbed Mt Millar (approx. 13,500ft)
	12th October	Climbed 'Mt Tyndall', thought to be Mt Brewer (13,570ft)
	15th October	First attempt on the 'supposed' Mt Whitney; actually climbed Mt Langley (14,000ft) and Mt Muir (14,500ft)
	29th October	First ascent of the eastern face of 'the real' Mt Whitney (14,494ft). Climbed 'throughout the Minarets'
1874	2nd November	Muir's first climb of Mt Shasta (14,400ft)
1875	28th April	Second climb of Mt Shasta with Geodetic Survey team
	30th April	Third climb of Mt Shasta with Jerome Fay
	23rd June	Ascent of Mt Joaquin
	10th November	Made the second ascent of South Dome, Yosemite
1877	3rd September	Climbed Mt Hamilton
1878	6th July	Climbed Mt Genson, Nevada
	13th July	Climbed Mt Grant, Nevada
	28th August	Climbed Lone Mountain, Death Valley. Also Mt Nebo, Mt Beaver and Wheelers Peak, Nevada
1879	July	First Alaskan Trip: Muir's first climb of Glenora Peak (8000ft) and his rescue of Samuel Hall Young
1880		Muir's second Alaska trip and second climb of Glenora, this time alone
	30th August	Adventure on the Taylor Glacier with 'Stickeen'
1888		Made the seventh recorded ascent of Mt Rainier led by Van Trump
1890	16th July	Camped on Muir Glacier, Glacier Bay
	18th July	Camped on summit of Quarry Mountain, Glacier Bay
	26th August	Climbed Mt Conners
1903		Climbs Mueller Glacier on Mount Cook, New Zealand.

JOHN MUIR
AND VERTICAL SAUNTERING

Arthur W Ewart

From *John Muir, Life and Work*, edited by Sally Miller.

> Something hidden. Go and find it.
> Go and look behind the ranges –
> Something lost behind the ranges
> Lost and waiting for you. Go!
> *Rudyard Kipling*

Right on the rim of Yosemite Valley, toes actually hanging out over the 3000-foot drop, John Muir could not '*help fearing a little that the rock might split off*', as he said. Overwhelmed by his first view of the valley from above, he backed off and ran around shouting, waving his arms and scaring off a bear with his frenzy. He had galloped westward along the rim in search of just such a place where he could look straight down. After drawing back from the lip he cautioned himself, 'now don't go out on the verge again'. But it was no use. In the face of such scenery 'one's body seems to go where it likes with a will over which we seem to have scarce any control', he said. Actually it was a glimpse of the falls that Muir really sought, so he followed Yosemite Creek down to the point where the water plunged over the abyss, and there he took off his boots and crept along the rushing water. The roar of the falls was deafening, but he was not quite able to peer over. He searched for some natural flaw in the smooth granite, hoping to climb still further out and gain a better view. 'Scanning it keenly,' he said, 'I discovered a narrow shelf about three inches wide on the very brink, just wide enough for a rest for one's heels.' He had second thoughts. The perch looked a little too 'nerve trying', he said. 'I therefore concluded not to venture farther.' No sooner had he decided against the attempt than he changed his mind again. Recognising a nearby plant as one quite caustic to the taste, he filled his mouth with the leaves, 'hoping they might help to prevent giddiness'. His mind thus distracted from thoughts of self-preservation and fear, Muir slipped his heels down onto the narrow shelf and moved slowly out to gain a perfect view of the water on its 1400-foot descent. Muir was enchanted, transfixed. He let his mind drift, trusting his body to do intuitively what was needed for safety, and he lost all sense of time.[1]

Aside from the many achievements that marked John Muir for immortality, he had another accomplishment less well publicised but equally distinguished. In the last quarter of the nineteenth century, John Muir was the best mountaineer in the United States. He set physical standards in the sport that are difficult to match today, and his mountaineering ethics have come to be appreciated and emulated only recently within the American climbing community.

A climber of legendary endurance, Muir moved with unparalleled finesse on vertical rock and ice. He had a string of mountain summits to his credit equalled by no other in his era. In sheer number of solitary ascents alone, Muir earned his title as the best mountaineer of his times. Yet pre-eminence as a climber is due him not so much for his physical prowess as for the personal philosophy he developed: a perspective on nature that he brought to the sport of climbing. To fully appreciate Muir the climber it is necessary not only to recount his feats but also to ask what motivated his efforts. No other climber was better at finding and becoming part of the harmony and perfection in the mountains, blending with the rocks, and revering them as teachers of God's design. Muir saw manifestations of God's intent everywhere he looked, and climbing to mountain summits was his way of finding that Spirit.

In the summer of 1869 Muir began a period of active mountaineering that spanned more than twenty-five years, and during that time he became not only an accomplished rock and ice climber, but also an all-round alpinist. With meagre provisions – usually just bread, tea, occasionally a little oatmeal – and a couple of blankets, Muir climbed peak after peak, alone most often; sometimes in bone-chilling, sub-freezing weather, in the face of formidable storms, and well beyond any hope of rescue.

' "Come higher",' Muir reported the mountain voices saying to him. 'Many still voices . . . are calling, "Come higher".'[2]

Weaned on harsh, demanding farm work in his youth and a lifestyle of puritanical frugality, Muir came to the mountains already armed with a determined will and leathery constitution. As one of his biographers said: 'He developed within himself a hard, stubborn core beyond the reach of any external situation'.[3] In many ways he led the life of an ascetic, deprived by most standards, but anything more to Muir seemed excessive luxury, appealing to the flesh while impeding the spirit. 'Just bread and water and delightful toil is all I need,' he said.[4] Refusing to care for himself in a conventional way, he actually enjoyed this life of privation. 'There is a weird charm in carrying out such a free and pathless plan,' he said of this method.[5] Muir attributed his pure physical drive to inherited qualities, his 'Scottish pluck and perseverance.'[6] That pluck allowed him to endure extreme hardship, to sleep out in his shirt-sleeves, often to go days without food in arduous situations that would break all but the most rugged souls.

California's Mount Whitney, the highest point in the contiguous United States, is not easily located by sight. It blends in with a number of other surrounding 14,000-foot peaks. On 15 October, 1873, when Muir set out alone to climb the mountain, the problem of finding it was compounded by the fact that in Clarence King's *Geological Survey of California*, upon which Muir relied, designation of the highest mountain had been conferred on the wrong peak. When Muir gained the summit he used his own elevation instrument to sight the real Whitney off in the distance. Setting out at once on foot, with no equipment, no blankets or food, he reached a 14,000-foot sub-peak just 500 feet below the summit of Whitney as darkness set in. It was extremely cold, Muir was sick, and, well above timber line, he had no wood for a fire. Here he spent a dreadful night and was able to keep warm only by staying in constant motion. 'I had to dance all night to keep from freezing,' he recalled, 'and was feeble and starving the next morning.'[7] At daybreak he attempted the summit again but was stopped by that 'other self' of which he sometimes spoke. This time it was clearly an audible voice that said 'Go back'. 'I felt as if Someone had caught me by the shoulder and turned me around,' he said.[8] He descended and walked all the way down to the town of Independence, a distance of about twenty miles. Replenished from a day of food and rest, he started out again on 19 October and walked up the easy canyon below the mountain. Ascending the east face, he arrived on the top of Whitney by 8 a.m. on the twenty-first, the first person ever to climb the mountain by that route. Despite the fact that he used 'small points of stones frozen . . . into the surface', for footholds, the route is not considered technically difficult by today's high standards of rock climbing.[9] Still, that does not diminish the arduousness of the whole experience. Francis Farquhar, historian of the Sierra Nevada, reminds us: 'Should someone of the present generation of mountain climbers feel inclined to make light of John Muir's exploit, let him endeavour to duplicate it, starting from Independence (not Lone Pine) on foot, with or without sleeping bag and concentrated foods.'[10]

The 1870s witnessed Muir's most intensive period of mountaineering. He roamed throughout the Sierra from Tahoe, south to Mount Whitney and north again to Mount Shasta. Characteristics of Muir's climbing style emerged in the early period: his reliance on minimal supplies (lacking even a rope, for example), the absence of self-glorification, and his unbridled enthusiasm for every adventure. Unabashed, he climbed talking out loud, whispering to flowers along the way, yelling, and gesticulating when he saw something particularly impressive. Muir had a spiritual love affair with everything wild, and he climbed to intensify his affection. 'Who wouldn't be a mountaineer?' he asked. 'Up here all the world's prizes seem nothing.'[11]

Living and working in Yosemite valley in the early 1870s he spent his Sundays scampering around his beloved valley. After he left his work as a sawyer and carpenter in 1871, he was free to 'saunter', as he called it, through the mountains in pursuit of his glacial studies, while all the time climbing day after day for long stretches. In 1872, Muir became the first and perhaps only American climber to be featured as a central figure in a work of fiction. The eccentric Thérése Yelverton, defrocked European countess and writer, visited Yosemite in search of material for her next book. She became enchanted with Muir. In her book, *Zanita: A Tale of the Yosemite*, he appeared as Kenmuir, a 'lithe figure . . . skipping over the rough boulders, poising with the balance of an athlete.'[12] Muir was affected by his encounter with Yelverton, slightly embarrassed by the adulation, but not nearly so moved by her as she was by him. And in later years, when he looked back on this year of his life, it was not the flirtation with a countess he recalled most vividly, but his epic climb of Mount Ritter in the Central Sierra.

The next year, 1873, was an especially productive climbing year for Muir. He climbed throughout the Minarets, the beautiful sub-range of peaks south of Yosemite; in the fall he completed the Whitney climb by way of what is now appropriately called the Mountaineer's Route. Muir was bursting with enthusiasm for his chosen sport after the Whitney ascent. He wrote to a friend, 'I saw no mountains in all this region that appeared at all inaccessible to a mountaineer. Give me a summer and a bunch of matches and a sack of meal and I will climb every one in the region.'[13] Muir was caught, captivated by the tonic that comes from adventure on high peaks, and he loved everything to do with the sport, even the hardships. He was coming to grips with himself, using the mountains and climbing as a means to search for himself. In his mid-thirties by this time, Muir was ready to state with certainty the one occupation he would always claim, 'I am hopelessly and forever a mountaineer.'[14]

Still half wild during this period, Muir resisted domestication, reluctantly coming down from the mountains only at the behest of his friends who implored him to share his knowledge. He relented in 1873, set up temporary residence in Oakland and spent ten months writing. It was his first extended period of confinement in six years, and he barely tolerated it. When he broke out finally in the fall of 1874, he shouted 'I'm wild once more,' and bolted for Yosemite Valley.[15] In November he was on top of Mount Shasta for the first time and after climbing the massive glacier-flanked peak, sat out a four-day storm camped on the side of the mountain. Local residents had given him up for lost. 'They thought that poor, crazy mountain climber must be frozen solid and lost below the drifts,' he later wrote.[16] In April 1875, he was again on Shasta, though this particular ascent nearly did cost him his life.

When the storm 'began to declare itself,' Muir recalled, he and his companion, Jerome Fay, were still on the summit of Mount Shasta completing a geodetic survey.[17] Fay, an employee of Justin Sisson who was a local hotel owner and major-domo of Shasta, had guided Muir part way up Shasta on the first ascent. Following that climb, Muir had extolled the mountain's virtues to a friend by saying 'The extent of its individuality is perfectly wonderful.'[18] Surely he and Fay must have also known that the severity of storms on the summits of singular mountains like Shasta was also distinctive. This one came on fast and ferocious, soon engulfing them in high winds and a severe hail shower. Still not alarmed, Muir took time to examine the hail's symmetry: 'six-sided pyramids with rounded base, rich and sumptuous looking, and fashioned with loving care'. With the situation rapidly deteriorating, descent that would take them entirely off the mountain seemed out of the question. Muir's thermometer registered below zero, the sky darkened, and lightning flashed simultaneously with ear-shattering thunder.

Muir was determined to walk off the mountain, but Fay was against the idea. Just below the summit, within the old volcanic core, there was then, on 30th April 1875, as today, a hot, bubbling fumarole pit where mud and steaming gases create a stark contrast to the ice that surrounds the hollow. This was where Fay decided to make his stand. Muir agreed: 'We can lie in the mud and steam and sludge, warm at least on one side.' This was no easy decision, for they committed themselves to wet clothes, the cardinal sin of mountaineering. They passed the night there. Two feet of snow fell in the first few hours. Their backs scalded in the hot mud as snow drifted over them 'augmenting our novel misery', said Muir. When the storm cleared, the temperature dropped even lower, and the two climbers talked to each other to keep from falling asleep and possibly dying. They began to hallucinate, seeing visions brought on by their 'dreamy stupor', and each hour passed as if it were a year. Finally day broke, and though it was still bitterly cold, they had to descend. Both climbers gulped down some whiskey left in Fay's flask, proving perhaps that Muir was uninhibited in the mountains if not always discriminate, and they began to stumble down the mountain. Both men had frozen feet and one of Muir's arms was numb, but they called upon 'a kind of second life, available only in emergencies'.

When they finally felt the warmth of the sun it renewed their will once more. Waiting for them as they reached timber line was Sisson who, knowing they were in trouble, had brought horses and provisions. It was the only time Muir ever had to be rescued in the mountains and he was glad for it. He convalesced with the help of the Sisson family, and regained full use of his arm but was slightly hobbled the rest of his life by those frozen feet that never fully recovered.

Muir continued his glacial studies and vertical adventures during his Alaskan trips, the first in 1879. But with his marriage to Louie Strentzel, the arrival of two daughters, and the demands of the family fruit ranch, Muir was sequestered at home in Martinez, California, for much of the 1880s. Finally in 1888, at age fifty, he broke out again, this time for good. He and a group of friends made the seventh recorded ascent of Mount Rainier in Washington. 'I did not mean to climb it,' he wrote, 'but got excited and soon was on top.'[19]

Approaching his sixtieth birthday in the mid-1890s, Muir showed no sign of retiring from the mountains. 'I must have been born a mountaineer,' he said in 1895, following a six-week trip to all his old haunts in the Sierra. 'I suppose old age will put an end to scrambling in rocks and ice, but I can still climb as well as ever.'[20] Even during his round-the-world tour of 1903–1904, when he was sixty-five, he was skilled enough to romp across the Mueller Glacier on Mount Cook in New Zealand, obviously enjoying himself, delighting in his continued agility. 'In jumping on the boulder-clad snout,' he wrote, 'I found my feet had not lost their cunning.'[21]

John Muir's climbing grit and unprecedented number of climbs during the era is impressive, but the ideas behind his achievements are still the most fascinating aspect of his mountaineering. When the focus is on Muir's thoughts, the philosopher-scientist-mountaineer is truly seen and the reason for his vertical quest becomes clear. Influenced by a background in the classics, the scriptures, and humanism, his driving force was essentially spiritual. One of America's foremost wilderness philosophers, with his own unique blend of mysticism, transcendentalism, pantheism, and mainstream Christianity, he was the only one to practise his philosophy on granite walls where even solid rock spoke to him. 'Religion is on all the rocks,' he said.[22] This inspiration brought an added dimension to Muir's exploits, and it is impossible to know the climber without understanding his spiritual preoccupation. When Muir looked at ice and rock, he saw something most of us miss. From the tiniest granite crystal to the most exalted, singular mountain monoliths, he heard and saw a 'Beauty', as he called it, that led him on, pulling him up into the world of vertical sauntering.

John Muir sensed more than silent, stoic beauty when he saw mountains; he felt brilliant, ebullient life bursting forth from the rock and ice. This vision affected all aspects of Muir's climbing and elevated his efforts from the realm of simple sport to spiritual quest. Mountains were not imposing barriers of inhospitable character, fraught with dangers, purposefully protected from assault by natural embattlements. Rather, they were gentle and had a message to convey to those who could intuitively sense their value. 'If I want the Sierra Mountain feeling on my back,' said Muir, 'I stand with my back to them as I would to a fire.'[23] Mountains and vertical cliffs were friendly and inviting to Muir, and he couldn't wait to make their acquaintance. 'When I reached Yosemite, all the rocks seemed talkative and more telling and loveable than ever,' he said. 'I love them with a love intensified by long and close companionship.'[24]

Muir felt a 'Spirit' speak in every whisper of wind on each summit, in movements of shadows cast across rock, in the intimate touch of cloud against rock, and in the piercing report of ice breaking away from the cliff. Nowhere was this relationship to the environment more obvious than in Muir's special cathedral, Yosemite Valley. 'No temple made with hands can compare with Yosemite. Every rock in its walls seems to glow with life,' he said.[25] The life he perceived in each crystal was a smaller, but no less magnificent, expression of the spirit he felt in the entire mountain range. When he designated the Sierras as the 'Range of Light', he was not acclaiming the illumination of the afternoon alpenglow but recognising the inspirational qualities of the whole range: an element of preternatural wisdom apparent to those who sought the 'good tidings' of the mountains. Intoxicated with this Beauty, Muir was swept into a dynamic interplay of physical environment and personal revelation, and he began to identify closely with the mountains and all their features.

'This I may say is the first time I have been at church in California,' said Muir after his climb of Cathedral Peak in the Sierra in the summer of 1869.[26] Several weeks earlier, when he first saw the peak he had hoped not to conquer it but to 'climb to it to say my prayers and hear the stone sermons.' Unbeknownst to Muir, his ascent of Cathedral Peak was the most difficult rock climb anyone had done in America.[27] Had he known what he was about to achieve in one of his first Yosemite climbs, he might have provided more of a literary drum roll, but as it was at the time, he stated simply, 'Left camp at daybreak and made direct for Cathedral Peak . . . which I reached at noon, having loitered by the way to study the fine trees.' Climbing by himself with no onlookers, no media to record the feat, Muir missed this opportunity for glory. Did he not know this was 1869 and he was in California, a land preoccupied with the heroic imperative, a place where people were chopping down the tallest, damming the wildest, building the biggest, extracting the most, and boasting of virility everywhere? Quite out of step for his time, Muir sensed only his diminutiveness, and awed by his reverence for everything wild, he felt no more important than all that was around him. Muir presented a counter-image for the Californians quite unlike that of the heroic conqueror. He became, according to Kevin Starr, all that the mountains themselves promised: 'simplicity, strength, joy, and affirmation', and he ultimately 'upgraded the entire Californian relationship to the mountains'.[28] Muir's confident steps toward Cathedral Peak were also some of his first steps toward becoming one of the most important figures in California history.

That a religious zeal permeated Muir's philosophy and his every move in the mountains should come as no surprise. Muir grew up hiding any book he read but the Bible from his harsh Calvinist father, but he memorised the entire Old Testament and much of the New. He never lost his love of the Bible for its beautiful prose or for its examples of life's ethical proprieties. Few people lived a more Christian life than did Muir, who ultimately came to peace with himself and rejected his father's God and embraced a more bene-volent deity, thereafter designated as 'Nature' or 'Beauty' or 'Spirit' in his writings. Influenced by his courses at the University of Wisconsin, his botany and geology classes, and especially by his friendship with

Jeanne Carr, wife of one of his professors, Muir was introduced to another world. Lyrical spokesmen for nature like Wordsworth and fellow Scotsman Robert Burns, coupled with the transcendentalists Thoreau and Emerson, convinced Muir that his particular vision of the world was not at odds with Christianity and that in fact, as he concluded, nature and the Bible 'harmonise beautifully'.[29] Later, in the midst of his Yosemite love affair he stated with confidence, 'Christianity and mountainanity are streams from the same fountain.'[30] America's foremost apostle of nature, Muir was on his own errand unto the wilderness, lending poignancy to his father's criticism.

Ultimately, Muir's religion, a kind of wilderness egalitarianism, had a significant effect on how he practised his sport of mountaineering, for he never sought to conquer the peaks, only to merge with them as equals. To a friend on the eve of her first visit to Yosemite he wrote, 'You'll find me as rough as the rocks and about the same colour – granite.'[31] What a sight he must have been for visitors to Yosemite as he returned from one of his mountain sojourns wearing his tattered clothes, his hair tangled, his face purposefully blackened to prevent burn, and forever skinny, having gone for days eating only bread, looking for all the world like some feral man. If there is a single-most important feature that separated John Muir from other climbers, it was his humility derived from his religion and his belief in the interdependence of all life. He had no wish to set himself apart, as some sovereign entity who could prove himself stronger than the mountains. Forever self-effacing, he never indulged in self-importance, he never bragged, and he certainly never left any physical evidence of his feats. 'I have never left my name on any mountain, rock, or tree in any wilderness,' he wrote in 1903.[32] Always respecting his Scots/Christian injunction against displays of vanity, indeed, Muir felt no pride in climbing a mountain only joy and a sense that he was a little closer to the 'Spirit' he sought on high peaks.

A final quality that separated Muir from other climbers once again was not his physical stamina, nor his technical finesse, but a sharply defined 'soul life', an intuition, a virtual sixth sense he developed in climbing. 'The life of a mountaineer seems to be particularly favourable to development of soul life,' he explained.[33] Speaking to him through his 'other self', this sense saved him in perilous situations, as on his first attempt of Mount Whitney, for example, and it always enabled him to climb beyond the point where others, bound by logic or reason, were stopped. This quality marked him off from more cerebral or purely physical climbers. Never was this characteristic more in evidence than on his ascent of Mount Ritter.

If a mountaineer truly presses himself to excel, sooner or later he will be faced with a seemingly insoluble and perilous situation high on a vertical face. Having exhausted his repertoire of physical and mental solutions to the difficulty, mild panic may set in, which only makes the predicament worse. Better climbers can keep this mental chaos at bay, but not for long. Logic is a poor partner at this point; reasoning fails the climber. In Muir's case, when this happened to him, he was on the face of Mount Ritter in the Sierra, and he recalled that his mind 'seemed to fill with a stifling smoke'.[34] By himself as usual, with no rope, his arms and legs spread-eagled on the rock and unable to move up or down, Muir was sure he was going to fall. Suddenly, inexplicably, he became 'possessed of a new sense. The other self – call it what you will . . . came forward and assumed control . . . and my limbs moved with a positiveness and precision with which I seemed to have nothing at all to do.' The danger passed, he continued on to the summit. Remaining on top almost until sunset, he was spellbound the entire time, his body reverberated from the new-found 'energy' that acutely heightened his senses.

In this episode, contemporary climbers see all the elements of a classic, epic climb: a first ascent, scaled on an unclimbed route, accomplished by a small, minimally equipped party; seemingly insurmountable danger skirted with the help of an intuitive sense. Finally, the climb ends on the summit with the climber in an altered state, experiencing a lucidity of mind and tranquillity of mood. This serenity is intoxicating, and will not let the climber leave the mountain top. Muir's ascent of Ritter had all these elements. There was no finer climb for him.[35]

More than once Muir came uncomfortably close to death in the mountains before escaping unharmed. On a number of occasions he was either lucky or had Someone watching over him. He made mistakes as does every mountaineer. Sometimes his judgement was poor, other times he was simply caught in reverie while nature was busy enveloping him in serenity. Never for a moment did be forget that he was mortal, but his religion removed the fear of dying in the mountains. 'Death is stingless indeed,' he said, 'and as beautiful as life itself.'[36] He even dreamt about his death several times. Once, what would have been a nightmare for most was accepted with equanimity by Muir. 'I dreamed I stood on the edge of a precipice shaken by an earthquake. The rock started to fall. I said, "Let us die calmly. This is a noble death".'[37] Another time, dreaming he fell from a cliff, he sensed himself 'rushing through the air'. Startled awake, he was both shaken and ecstatic, and he shouted: 'Where could a mountaineer find a more glorious death?'[38] Muir never wanted to die while climbing, but he accepted that possibility as the price for getting that much closer to the Beauty he knew was most conspicuous in high places.

Samuel Hall Young, Alaskan missionary, friend and occasional climbing partner of John Muir, was not quite as blasé about his own mortality as was Muir. Faced with the imminent possibility of his death on Glenora Peak, high above the Stickeen River in Alaska, Young found himself reviewing his life, thinking of his pregnant wife, and wondering how long the fall would last before he hit the glacier below.[39]

This occurred after Muir, on his first trip by steam ship to Alaska, met Young who was in the company of some renowned missionaries. When the steamer tied up for the day at Glenora, the Captain told all the passengers to amuse themselves. Muir came to life. 'I saw Muir's eyes light up across the table,' said Young. The evangelist was in a fix, however, having to defer to his superiors who, as he remembered 'had a special mission to suppress all my self-destructive proclivities toward dangerous adventure, and especially to protect me from "that wild Muir" and his hare-brained schemes of mountain climbing.' With the enticement of an 8000-foot peak, ten miles away, Muir had a goal for the day and was impatient. Young, using a little 'guile', devised a way to elude his elders for the day, and soon he and Muir were off.

The climb went fairly well with Muir stopping to talk to flowers in a 'curious mixture of scientific lingo and baby talk', Young said. He marvelled at Muir's climbing ability and swore that Muir had some sort of negative gravity machine strapped to his back. Still, Young managed to keep up with him until a fall, where the venture took a sharp turn from light-hearted to serious.

Muir was climbing slightly ahead of Young and had reached the summit unaware of his partner's predicament. Backtracking, he came upon Young and was startled. 'My God!' he cried when he saw him. Young had tried to launch himself across a small gap, but slipped and made a desperate lunge for the other side. The fall dislocated both of Young's shoulders, and though he landed on a small ledge, he was gradually slipping off. When Muir spotted him he instantly reassured Young. 'Hold fast; I'm going to get you out of this.' Unable to reach Young from his advanced position, Muir crossed behind the peak and arrived just above his partner.

By that time, Young was almost over the edge and, with the pain in his shoulder almost unbearable, had nearly given up. Muir crept down to him, holding onto the rock with one hand, reached down, and grabbed Young by the belt with the other hand. With Young's feet providing some grip on the rock, Muir pulled the fallen climber up and out over the sheer drop. 'My head swung down, my impotent arms dangling,' remembered Young. Muir pulled him up close, caught his collar with his teeth, and managed to bring him to rest on a small ledge where they were both temporarily safe.

What followed was a nightmare for the two as they were still a thousand feet above the glacier, with no rope, as always, and ten miles from the ship once they got off the vertical rock. The temperature was quite cold, the sun was just setting, and neither had a coat. Standing on that small ledge, Muir worked on Young's shoulders and was able to get the right arm back into its socket, restoring partial use. The left arm, however, was much worse, with the head of the bone thrust up into Young's armpit: it could not be reset. The two began a night-long descent. Muir would lower himself and then Young would slip down on top of him. Young's worst arm was in a sling, and the other, his right, offered some support, though it popped out three more times during their struggle to reach the ship.

When they reached the glacier below, the ten remaining miles seemed impossible, but the pair laboured on, Muir 'always cheery, full of talk', said Young. He cracked jokes while working tirelessly, lowering Young down the gravel slopes and throwing water in his face when Young was about to faint. By daylight they were back at the ship to find the grim, senior missionaries staring down at them from the deck.

The catalogue of John Muir's mountaineering exploits continues, each story revealing a little more about this consummate climber and each adding to a well-deserved legend. Norman Foerster, in his work *Nature in American Literature*, wrote of Muir: 'Never, perhaps, had there been such a complete mountaineer and glacier climber as he, unsurpassed alike in skill, in knowledge, in passionate enjoyment.'[40] Muir was the first well-known climber in America to realise that the object of the sport was not *what* you climbed, but *how* you climbed: means were more important than ends, finesse more important than force. Climbing was part of Muir's religion, not mere egotistical diversion; he simply brought body and spirit to the vertical world – not mounds of equipment, rock hammers, or bolts to be driven into the rock. It has taken American climbers a hundred years to understand what Muir was talking about when he said 'It is astonishing how high and far we can climb in the mountains that we love and how little we require food and clothing.'[41] Climbing demands a certain humility in the face of the superiority of Nature, and an acknowledgement that brute strength and advanced equipment will only take one so far in the mountains. There is a proper way to climb, the image of the rugged individualist making his own rules in the wilderness notwithstanding, and Muir knew this a century before the ethical craze hit the American climbing scene in the early 1970s. Suddenly then – exposing their puritan roots – American climbers became consumed with moral imperatives about the proper way to climb and imposed injunctions against harming the rock with excessive equipment.

Muir was a climbing purist, the founding father of 'clean climbing' in this country, and the best climber of his era. The virtues he brought to the sport – intellect, determination, perseverance, spirituality, and the desire to understand divine manifestations – made him the sport's foremost Renaissance man. We can confer this title upon him not simply by looking at his ideas or by recounting his feats, but by studying the juncture between his ideas and his actions. No armchair transcendentalist, no cloistered seminarian, he was out in the world searching for God and showing the way for others, intensely involved in both spiritual pursuit and civic responsibility. The success of the Sierra Club is testimony to his efforts in the latter, and his own words leave little doubt that he achieved his vision quest. 'When the glorious summits are gained, the weariness all vanishes in a moment as the vast landscapes of white mountains are beheld reposing in the sky, every peak with its broad flowing folds of white, glowing in God's sunshine, serene and silent, devout like a human being. This is true transportation.'[42]

It is painful to think of John Muir, on the night of 24 December, 1914, dying in that hospital bed rather than among his friends, the mountains. There is stark contrast between the image of the young, powerful climber earlier in his life and the coughing, lonely figure close to death still trying to spread the Word, his notes for his next book at hand. But Muir survives in the power of his mountaineering legacy, and the virtues he possessed as a climber were not simply means for scaling icy peaks or granite cliffs but also guidelines for living.

'The mountains are calling and I must go.'[43] – John Muir

NOTES AND REFERENCES

1. Details of this account on the rim of Yosemite Valley, and Muir's words, are taken from John Muir, *My First Summer in the Sierra* (1911; reprinted Houghton Mifflin, Boston 1979), pp.115–121.
2. Ibid., p.86.
3. Stephen Fox, *John Muir and His Legacy: The American Conservation Movement* (Little, Brown, Boston 1981), p.34.
4. Muir, *First Summer*, p.78.
5. John Muir, quoted in William Frederic Badè, *The Life and Letters of John Muir*, 2 vols. (Houghton Mifflin, Boston 1924), I, p.311.
6. John Muir, letter to Mrs. Daniel Muir, 16 November, 1871, in Ibid., p.315.
7. John Muir, *John of the Mountains: the Unpublished Journals of John Muir*, Linnie Marsh Wolfe (ed.) (1938; reprinted University of Wisconsin Press, Madison 1979), p.187.
8. John Muir quoted in Linnie Marsh Wolfe, *Son of the Wilderness: The Life of John Muir* (1945; reprinted University of Wisconsin Press, Madison 1979), p.169.
9. John Muir, correspondence to *San Francisco Bulletin*, reprinted in Robert Engberg, *John Muir: Summering in the Sierra* (University of Wisconsin Press, Madison 1984), p.110.

10. Francis Farquhar, 'The Story of Mt Whitney,' *Sierra Club Bulletin* (1935); Steve Roper credits Muir with the first ascent: Roper, *Climber's Guide to the High Sierra* (Sierra Club Books, San Francisco 1976), p.368.
11. Muir, *First Summer*, p.53.
12. Therese Yelverton Longsworth, *Zanita: A Tale of the Yosemite* (Hurd and Houghton, New York 1872), pp.5–8.
13. John Muir, letter to Jeanne Carr, 13 October, 1874, in Badè, *Life and Letters*, I, pp.393–394.
14. Ibid., 7 October, 1874, p.28.
15. Muir, quoted in Wolfe, *Son of the Wilderness*, p.176.
16. John Muir, letter to JB McChesney, 9 November, 1874, in Badè, *Life and Letters*, II, p.35.
17. Details of the Shasta climb and Muir's quotes, unless otherwise noted, are found in John Muir, *Steep Trails*, edited by William Frederic Badè (Houghton Mifflin, New York 1918), pp.57–81.
18. Muir, letter to Jeanne Carr, 1 November 1874, in Badè, *Life and Letters*, II, p.31.
19. Muir, quoted in Badè, *Life and Letters*, II, pp.219–220.
20. Ibid., pp.290–291.
21. Muir, quoted in Wolfe, *Son of the Wilderness*, p.299.
22. Ibid., p.144
23. John Muir, letter to John and Maggie Reid, 13 January, 1869, p.8.
24. Muir, *Steep Trails*, pp.19–20.
25. John Muir, *The Yosemite* (1912; reprinted Sierra Club Books, San Francisco 1989), p.34.
26. Details of the Cathedral Peak climb, as well as Muir's quotes, are taken from *First Summer*, pp.198, 247–250.
27. For this determination, I have relied upon the judgement of Steve Roper, *The Climber's Guide to the High Sierra*, p.13. Roper also credits Muir with the first ascent of Cathedral Peak (p.334).
28. Kevin Starr, *Americans and the California Dream* (Oxford University Press, New York 1973), p.184.
29. John Muir, letter to Jeanne Carr, 21 January, 1866. In John Muir, *Letters to a Friend*, (1915, reprinted Norman S Burg, Dunwoody 1973), p.1.
30. John Muir, letter to JB McChesney, 10 January 1883, in Badè, *Life and Letters*, I, p.378.
31. John Muir, letter to Emily Pelton, 2 April, 1872, in Muir, *Letters to a Friend*, I, p.325.
32. Muir, quoted in Badè, *Life and Letters*, I, p.396.
33. Muir, *John of the Mountains*, p.77.
34. Details of the Ritter climb, as well as Muir's quotes, are found in Muir, *The Mountains of California* (1894; reprinted Dorset Press, New York 1988), pp.52–74.

35. That Muir made the first ascent of Ritter is cited in Roper, *Climber's Guide to the High Sierra*, p.336.
36. John Muir, *Thousand Mile Walk* (Houghton Mifflin, Boston 1915), p.71.
37. Muir, *John of the Mountains*, p.125.
38. Muir, *First Summer*, p.121.
39. Details of the Glenora Peak climb and quotes from Young are found in S Young Hall, *Alaska Days with John Muir* (Fleming Revell Company, New York 1912), pp.11–56. Muir was somewhat embarrassed by the publicity from this and other glamorised accounts of the climb, and wrote his own version. Still, the essential facts remained unchanged.
40. Norman Foerster, *Nature in American Literature* (Russell and Russell, New York 1958), p.243.
41. Muir, *John of the Mountains*, p.69.
42. Ibid., p.329.
43. John Muir, letter to Sarah Galloway, 3 September, 1873, in Badè, *Life and Letters*, I, p.385.

2

JOHN MUIR
AND THE RANGE OF LIGHT

Francis P Farquhar

from *History of the Sierra Nevada*

Then it seemed to me the Sierra should be called not the
Nevada or Snowy Range, but the Range of Light. And after
ten years spent in the heart of it, rejoicing and wondering,
bathing in the glorious floods of light, seeing the sunbursts
of morning among the icy peaks, the noonday radiance on
the trees and rocks and snow, the flush of the alpenglow
and a thousand dashing waterfalls with their marvellous
abundance of irised spray, it still seems to me above all
others the Range of Light, the most divinely beautiful of all
the mountain chains I have ever seen.
John Muir

To Muir all was order and beauty, from the grandest features of the
sculptured mountains to the minutest flowers. Instead of theorising
about origins and processes he examined the results in all their
smallest detail, following streams upward to their sources, looking
critically into the structure of rocks. His conclusions were based on
observed phenomena, which led him to declare: 'In the beginning of
the long glacial winter, the lofty Sierra seems to have consisted of one
vast undulated wave, in which a thousand separate mountains, with
their domes and spires, their innumerable canyons and lake basins,
lay concealed. In the development of these, the Master Builder chose
for a tool, not the earthquake nor lightning to rend asunder, not the
stormy torrent nor eroding rain, but the tender snow-flowers, noise-
lessly falling through unnumbered seasons, the offspring of the sun
and sea.'[1]

With allowance for the exuberance of discovery and the exalted vision of a poet, Muir's concept of the development of the Sierra by orderly process and predetermined forms was far nearer the truth as now conceived than the pronouncements of the learned scientist, Professor Whitney, who declared that 'a more absurd theory was never advanced than that by which it was sought to ascribe to glaciers the sawing out of these vertical walls and the rounding of the domes. This theory, based on entire ignorance of the whole subject, may be dropped without wasting any more time upon it. The theory of erosion not being admissible to account for the formation of Yosemite valley, we have to fall back on one of those movements of the earth's crust to which the primal forms of the mountain valleys are due.' In short, 'the bottom of the valley sank down to an unknown depth, owing to the support being withdrawn from underneath, during some of those convulsive movements which must have attended the upheaval of so extensive and elevated a chain.' Muir was called 'a mere sheepherder, an ignoramus.'[2]

But the 'sheepherder' had eyes to see and vision far beyond that of a pedant. His was no superficial geology, but a patient, persistent search for truth evolved from the evidence before him. There were no imaginary cataclysms, no catastrophes of Nature. Everything that Muir saw testified to orderly processes that exemplified eternal Principle. 'Such is Yosemite,' he wrote, 'the noblest of Sierra temples, everywhere expressing the working of Divine harmonious law, yet so little understood that it has been regarded as an "exceptional creation", or rather exceptional destruction accomplished by violent and mysterious forces.'[3]

How did it come about that John Muir, the 'sheepherder', attained such insight? He was indeed momentarily a sheepherder, but that occupation merely a fortuitous excuse for reaching a desired goal. The young Scotsman – he was then thirty years old – had made a brief visit to Yosemite immediately upon his arrival in California in 1868 and could hardly wait for an opportunity to return to the Sierra. The following year the opportunity occurred when a sheep rancher, Pat Delaney, offered Muir the job of taking sheep to the high country to escape the summer drought. He had merely to act as a supervisor; an experienced sheepman and a good sheepdog would take care of the daily routine. It was agreed that Muir should have plenty of time for studying plants and rocks and scenery.

Most of the months of June and July were spent in the region of Yosemite Creek, with climbs of Mount Hoffmann and North Dome, and a quick trip to Yosemite valley. There was an experience at the brink of Yosemite Fall not recommended for neophytes of less nerve than Muir: 'I took off my shoes and stockings and worked my way cautiously down alongside the rushing flood, keeping my feet and hands pressed firmly on the polished rock. The booming, roaring water, rushing past close to my head, was very deafening.' He wanted to get down farther where he could see the full length of the fall.

The slope looked dangerously smooth and steep, and the rushing flood beneath, overhead, and beside me was very nerve trying. I therefore concluded not to venture farther, but did nevertheless. Tufts of artemisia were growing in clefts of rock nearby, and I filled my mouth with the bitter leaves, hoping they might help to prevent giddiness. Then with a caution not known in ordinary circumstances, I crept down safely to the little ledge. Here I obtained a perfectly free view down into the heart of the chanting throng of comet-like streamers, into which the body of the fall soon separates.[4]

He moved on with the sheep to the Tuolumne Meadows. He climbed Mount Dana and descended Bloody Canyon to Mono Lake. The climax was an ascent of Cathedral Peak, during which he seems to have taken equal interest in the abundance of flowers and the structure of the peak.

The body of the Cathedral is nearly square and the roof slopes are wonderfully regular and symmetrical, the ridge trending northeast and southwest. This direction has apparently been determined by structure joints in the granite. The gable on the northeast end is magnificent in size and simplicity. The front is adorned with many pinnacles and a tall spire of curious workmanship. Here too the joints in the rock are seen to have played an important part in determining their forms and size and general arrangement.'

And in contrast, 'here at last in front of the Cathedral is blessed cassiope, ringing her thousands of sweet-toned bells, the sweetest church music I ever enjoyed.'[5] Thus did Muir characteristically mingle the senses, rejoicing in whatever expressed order and beauty.

Muir summarises the results of his first summer:

> The best gains of this trip were the lessons of unity and inter-relation of all the features of the landscape revealed in general views. The lakes and meadows are located just where the ancient glaciers bore heaviest at the foot of the steepest parts of their channels, and of course their longest diameters are approximately parallel with the belts of forests growing in long curving lines on the lateral and medial moraines, and in broad outspreading fields on the terminal beds deposited toward the end of the ice period when the glaciers were receding. How interesting everything is! Every rock, mountain, stream, plant, lake, forest, garden, bird, beast, insect seems to call and invite us to come and learn something of its history and relationship.[6]

Although at the moment he did not see how he could accept this invitation, nevertheless, so strong was the call that he did find a way and spent the next six years continuously and intensively studying these rocks and plants and birds, even insects, so enthralling were the lessons they taught him.

Yosemite drew Muir as if by a magnet. In November of that year, 1869, he made his way to the Valley and applied to Hutchings for a subsistence job, as he expressed it, 'to feed sows and turkeys, build hen-roosts, laying-boxes, etc. Also to take charge of the ladies and to build a sawmill.'[7] The ladies that first year seem to have consisted of young Mrs Elvira Hutchings, in whom Muir found a companionate lover of flowers; Florence, five-year-old daughter of the house (she was the first white child born in Yosemite), 'a little black-eyed witch of a girl', whom he nicknamed 'Squirrel'; and Mrs Sproat, Elvira's mother, 'nurse, cook, and domestic manager of hotel and home', who made 'memorable muffins', In such company John passed a glorious snow-bound winter with enough time off from his duties to explore the Valley and its walls and to build for himself a cabin on Yosemite Creek. 'Near where it first gathers its beaten waters at the foot of the fall, I dug a small ditch and brought a stream into the cabin, entering at one end and flowing out the other with just current enough to allow it to sing and warble in low, sweet tones, delightful at night while I lay in bed.'[8]

Spring came slowly, interrupted by snowstorms now and then, which only served to expand the falls to greater grandeur when the sun shone again. Soon Muir was making quick excursions to the heights. On 27 June he writes in his journal, 'Arose betimes and walked to the top of Sentinel Dome. Had a fine view of the ever-glorious Sierra crest. I walked to Starr King, passing the old moraine on the banks of Illilouette Fall. And I walked above Nevada Fall into Little Yosemite. I made a memorable descent of the Nevada cliff on the left.'[9] Two days later he again went to Sentinel Dome, with Judge Colby,[10] and camped and saw the sunrise. And now came the tourists, to whom he expounded his glacier theories, in contradiction of the pronouncements of the State Geologist. One extraordinary tourist came that summer and saw so much in humans as well as scenery that she settled down to write a novel. Therése Yelverton, who claimed with good sanction to be Viscountess Avonmore, saw so much that was unusual and romantic in the persons of John Muir and little Florence Hutchings that she made them the hero and heroine of her novel, which she called *Zanita* (an improvised contraction of *manzanita*), raising her heroine to a maturity far beyond her years and an endowment beyond plausibility. 'Kenmuir', the hero, was a curious blend of fact and distortion. She describes him, 'with open blue eyes of honest questioning, and glorious auburn hair. His figure was about five feet nine, well knit, and bespoke the active grace which only trained muscles can assume.' A few snatches of conversation throughout the novel indicate that Muir was avidly preaching his glacial doctrines, but for the most part the depiction of life in Yosemite in 1870 is obscured and distorted by insufferable absurdities that make the book almost unreadable. An episode outside the novel, however, brings us back to real life. The *Mariposa Gazette* of 10 November, 1870, reports: 'The Hon. Mrs Yelverton met with a serious misfortune on Sunday last in attempting to leave Yosemite Valley unattended.' Two men travelling the Wawona trail noticed a woman's tracks in the snow leading away from the trail. Mrs

Yelverton was finally found, 'wet, chilled, bewildered and exhausted about a quarter of a mile from where she had left the trail. It is supposed Mrs Yelverton became bewildered in the snow storm of Sunday afternoon, and she could no longer manage her horse, and dismounted and tried to walk back, but lost her way, and wandered till exhausted.' Not long afterward, when she had recovered, she was escorted to Mariposa and went on to San Francisco. She wrote to Muir, who had temporarily left the Valley, chiding him for not waiting to guide her out. Muir felt 'a kind of guiltiness in not doing so', but it may be that the wary Scot had fled in embarrassment, as is suggested by a later letter from far away, in which she wrote:

My dear Kenmuir, how I wished for you, and sometimes longed for you avails me not to say. It is sufficient to make you comprehend that I never see a beautiful flower or a fine combination in nature without thinking of you and wishing you were there to appreciate it with me. One of the critics of *Zanita* says that your character is all 'bosh' and exists in my imagination. I should like to tell him that you had an existence in my heart as well![11]

Of greater significance in the history of the Sierra Nevada, and more in keeping with, John Muir's nature, was the arrival in August of the 'University Excursion Party', a group of young men from the University of California who had invited their geology professor, Joseph LeConte, to accompany them on a camping trip.[12] While exploring the Valley, they stopped a moment at the foot of the Yosemite Falls, at a sawmill, to make inquiries. 'Here we found a man in rough miller's garb, whose intelligent face and earnest, clear blue eyes excited our interest. After some conversation, we discovered it was John Muir, a gentleman of whom we had heard much from Mrs Professor Carr and others. We urged him to go with us to Mono, and he seemed disposed to do so.' A few days later Muir joined the party, affording many opportunities for sympathetic discussions about glaciers and rock formations. At Tenaya Lake one evening there took place a tableau of supreme piquancy: 'After supper,' writes LeConte, 'I went with Mr Muir and sat on a rock jutting into the lake. It was full moon. I never saw a more delightful scene. The deep stillness of the night; the silvery light and deep shadows of the mountains; the reflection on the water, broken into thousands of glittering points by the ruffled surface; the gentle lapping of the wavelets upon the rocky shore – all these seemed exquisitely harmonised with one another and the grand harmony made answering music in our hearts. Gradually the lake surface became quiet and mirror-like, and the exquisite surrounding scenery was seen double. For an hour we remained sitting in silent enjoyment of this delicious scene, which we reluctantly left to go to bed.' They continued to Tuolumne Meadows, made a climb of Mount Dana, and went down Bloody Canyon to Mono Lake and the Craters, where Muir left the party to return to Yosemite. The professor shortly afterwards published several articles in which he expressed views substantially in agreement with those of Muir about glaciation and rock structure. In neither does there appear to have been any thought of rivalry; no doubt each contributed to the development of the other's ideas and together they spread a doctrine that gained wider acceptance than the theories so stubbornly maintained by the Whitney school.

John Muir was by now thoroughly committed to his wilderness life. Yosemite was his home. Hutchings had taken over his cabin, so he constructed a 'hang-nest' high on the side of the sawmill, where he could keep his personal things and at the same time tend the mill. Here he could enjoy 'the piney fragrance of the fresh-sawn boards and be in constant view of the grandest of all the falls.' But he did not spend all his time at the mill, nor all his nights in his hang-nest; he was not what could be called a steady workman. He found a ledge high up beside Yosemite Fall, where he established a comfortable perch after a preliminary drenching from the swaying column. There, and on brief excursions to the upper country, he continued to muse upon glaciers.

One day in May, 1871, the distinguished poet and essayist, Ralph Waldo Emerson, arrived in the Valley with an escort of Bostonians who hung upon his every word. There had been letters of introduction, but Muir was too diffident to present himself in person, so left a note at Hutchings' hotel. Next day Emerson sought out the writer and found him at the sawmill. Cordiality was immediate. Muir invited him to his hang-nest, 'not easy of access, being reached only by a series of sloping planks roughened by slats like a hen ladder; but he bravely climbed up and I showed him my collection of plants and sketches, which seemed to interest him greatly.' Emerson invited Muir to accompany him to the Mariposa Grove of Big Trees, and Muir accepted with the urgent stipulation that they camp out beneath the giant trees. Emerson was enthusiastic, but his friends 'would have none of it, and held Mr Emerson to the hotels and trails. "It would never do to lie out in the night air – Mr Emerson might take cold." Sad commentary on culture and the glorious transcendentalism.' They did visit the Grove, however, and Emerson was impressed, 'but he was past his prime, and was now in the hands of his affectionate but sadly civilised friends, who seemed as full of old-fashioned conformity as of bold intellectual independence. The party rode away in wondrous contentment. I followed to the edge of the grove. Emerson lingered, turned his horse, took off his hat and waved me a last good-bye. After sundown I built a great fire, and as usual had it all to myself.'[13]

For some time Muir and Hutchings had not been getting along together, nor could it have been otherwise. Their daily objectives as well as their concepts of life were completely divergent. So Muir quit the sawmill work, left Hutchings, and moved his small store of personal things down the Valley to Black's Hotel. But the confines of the Valley would no longer contain him and from now on he began to move in ever-widening circles. During the summer of 1871 he was constantly among the higher mountains. His first objective was a search for evidences of ancient glaciers in the region of Yosemite Creek, up to its sources under Mount Hoffmann; then, evidences of the ancient Tuolumne Glacier in the region of mounts Lyell and Dana. In all this he was abundantly rewarded. In September he made a thrilling descent into the heart of the great Tuolumne Canyon.[14] He then turned his attention to the other side of the Valley. He climbed Mount Clark, where he beheld a glorious sunset. And now came his greatest reward.[15] 'On one of the yellow days of October, 1871, when I was among the mountains of the Merced group, following the footprints of the ancient glaciers that once flowed grandly from their ample fountains, reading what I could of their history as written in moraines, canyons, lakes and carved rocks, I came upon a small stream that was carrying mud of a kind I had never seen. Then I observed that this muddy stream issued from a bank of fresh quarried stones and dirt. This I at once took to be a moraine. When I had scrambled to the top of the moraine, I saw what seemed to be a huge snow-bank, four or five hundred yards in length, by half a mile in width. Imbedded in its stained and furrowed surface were stones and dirt like those of which the moraine was built. Dirt-stained lines curved across the snow-bank from side to side, and when I observed these curved lines with the moraine, and that the stones and dirt were most abundant near the bottom of the bank, I shouted, ' "A living glacier!" ' He made a thorough exploration of his new-found glacier, finding at its head a crevasse of clear, green ice. The following year he returned to Mount Lyell, and with Galen Clark's assistance made measurements of the movement of the Lyell and Maclure glaciers. He was then satisfied to publish announcements of his findings. Professor LeConte went to Mount Lyell and observed the evidences and concurred that there was true glacial motion. But acceptance of Muir's discovery was not immediately unanimous. Whitney continued obdurate. 'It may be stated,' he says in his ultimate publication on the Sierra, 'that there are no glaciers at all in the Sierra Nevada',[16] and Clarence King gave what he considered a final verdict: 'In the dry season of 1864-5 the writer examined many of the regions described by Mr Muir in the Sierra Nevada, and in not a few cases his so-called glaciers had entirely melted away. The absurdity of applying the word "glacier" to a snow-mass which appears and reappears from year to year will be sufficiently evident. Motion alone is no proof of a true glacier.'[17] There is nothing here to show that King examined the same places that Muir did, or if he did, that he gave them the same careful attention. The conceited 'scientist' had actually no more claim to that designation than had John Muir, if as much, and he was certainly not justified in the sneering remark he appended to his statement: 'It is to be hoped that Mr Muir's vagaries will not deceive geologists who are personally unacquainted with California, and that the ambitious amateur himself may divert his evident enthusiastic love of nature into a channel, if there is one, in which his attainments would save him from hopeless floundering.' These patronising words, coupled with the 'sheepherder' appellation, may be consigned to burial in glacial mud. Modern geologists agree substantially with John Muir and recognise him as the discoverer of living glaciers in the Sierra Nevada.[18]

It is not easy to follow John Muir's movements from his writings, nor even from his notebooks. He was not much concerned with calendars and dates. There are indications that he climbed Mount Lyell in the fall of 1871, and he has been credited with making the first ascent. But his time that fall is quite well accounted for until the glacier discovery in October, and before that others had reached the summit. Hutchings states that he had found the card of a Mr Tileston, of Boston, on the summit some ten days after it had been left.[19] The solitary climber proved to be a young man named John Boies Tileston, whose letters, printed long afterwards, contain the following passage:

> On Monday, the 28th August, 1871, we moved camp to the foot of Mt Lyell. After dinner I decided to begin the ascent on that day, so as to be on the snow in the morning before it should be softened by the sun. So I took my blankets and provisions, and set out at four. I walked up till it was nearly dark, when I found a comfortable place to sleep. I found some dry wood not far off, where some stunted pines grew in crevices of the rock, made some tea in a tin cup, and enjoyed the strange and savage scene around me. Immense precipices, great masses of snow, from which rose the black peaks of the summit, the roar of water descending by many channels and cascades over and among the rocks, and occasionally the rattling down of loosened stones, and the novelty of my situation, alone in that wild place, made a scene which impressed itself on my mind. I was up early the next morning, toasted some bacon, boiled my tea, and was off at six. I climbed the mountain, and reached the top of the highest pinnacle ('inaccessible', according to the State Geological Survey), before eight. I came down the mountain, and reached camp before one, pretty tired.[20]

John Muir seems to have climbed Mount Lyell in 1872, but whether for the first or second time is not clear. He spent some time measuring the Lyell and Maclure glaciers. On his return from one of his trips he found three artists waiting for him at his new cabin at the foot of the Royal Arches. One of the artists was William Keith. Did Muir know of any place in the high mountains suitable for a picture? He knew just the place. 'I saw it only yesterday,' he said. 'The crown of the Sierra is a picture hung in the sky, and mind you, it needs none of your selection, or "composition". I'll take you there tomorrow.'[21]

It was late in the season, so they lost no time. Muir led them out of the Valley by way of the Nevada Fall trail and the Merced–Tuolumne divide. 'The general expression of the scenery–rocky and savage-seemed sadly disappointing; and as they threaded the forest from ridge to ridge, eagerly scanning the landscapes as they were unfolded, [the artists] said "all this is huge and sublime, but we see nothing as yet at all available for effective pictures." . . . "Never mind,' I replied, 'only bide a wee'. At length, toward the end of the second day, the Sierra crown began to come into view and the whole picture stood revealed in the full flush of the alpen glow. Now their enthusiasm was excited beyond bounds. Here, at last, was a typical alpine landscape.' While the artists settled down happily at the Lyell Fork to sketch and paint, Muir decided to make an 'excursion to the untouched summit of Ritter'. He warned the artists not to be alarmed if he failed to appear before a week or ten days.

'My general plan,' writes Muir,[22] 'was . . . to scale the canyon wall, cross over to the eastern flank of the range, and then make my way southward to the northern spurs of Mount Ritter. My first day was pure pleasure . . . crossing the dry pathways of the ancient glaciers, tracing happy streams, and learning the habits of the birds and marmots.' Mount Ritter was still miles away when night came. He made his bed in a 'nook of the pine thicket, where the branches were pressed and crinkled overhead like a roof, and bent down around the sides'. He had to creep out to the fire often during the night, 'for it was biting cold and I had no blankets'.

> Breakfast of bread and tea was soon made. I fastened a hard, durable crust to my belt [and] set forth free and hopeful . . . immediately in front loomed the majestic mass of Mount Ritter, with a glacier swooping down its face nearly to my

feet, then curving westward and pouring its frozen flood into a dark blue lake . . . I began instinctively to scrutinise every notch and gorge and weathered buttress of the mountain, with reference to making the ascent . . . I succeeded in gaining the foot of the cliff on the eastern extremity of the glacier, and discovered the mouth of a narrow avalanche gully . . .

Its general course is oblique to the plane of the mountain-face, and the metamorphic slates of which the mountain is built are cut by cleavage planes in such a way that they weather off in angular blocks, giving rise to irregular steps that greatly facilitate climbing . . . The situation was becoming gradually more perilous, but, having passed several dangerous spots, I dared not think of descending . . . At length . . . I found myself at the foot of a sheer drop in the bed of the avalanche channel . . . which absolutely seemed to bar all further progress . . . The tried dangers beneath seemed even greater than that of the cliff in front; therefore, after scanning its face again and again, I began to scale it, picking my holds with intense caution. After gaining a point about halfway to the top, I was suddenly brought to a dead stop, with arms outspread, clinging close to the face of the rock, unable to move hand or foot either up or down. My doom appeared fixed. I *must* fall.

When this final danger flashed in upon me, I became nerve-shaken for the first time since setting foot on the mountain, and my mind seemed to fill with a stifling smoke. But this terrible eclipse lasted only a moment, when life blazed forth again with preternatural clearness. I seemed suddenly to become possessed of a new sense. The other self, bygone experiences, Instinct, or Guardian Angel – call it what you will – came forward and assumed control. Then my trembling muscles became firm again, every rift and flaw was seen as through a microscope, and my limbs moved with a positiveness and precision with which I seemed to have nothing at all to do. Had I been borne aloft upon wings, my deliverance could not have been more complete.

Above this memorable spot, the face of the mountain is still more savagely hacked and torn . . . But the strange influx of strength I had received seemed inexhaustible. I found a way without effort, and soon stood upon the topmost crag in the blessed light.

Muir gazed down upon 'giant mountains, valleys innumerable, glaciers and meadows, rivers and lakes, with the wide blue sky bent tenderly over them all, and in contemplation of Nature's methods of landscape creation. But in the midst of these fine lessons and landscapes, I had to remember that the sun was wheeling far to the west, while a new way had to be discovered, at least to some point of the timberline where I could have fire; for I had not even burdened myself with a coat.' After a look at the western side, he scrambled back to the head of a glacier flowing northeast. Down this he found a way. 'Night drew near before I reached the eastern base of the mountain, and my camp lay many a rugged mile to the north. Darkness came on, but I found my way by the trend of the canyons and the peaks projected against the sky. All excitement died with the light, and then I was weary. But the joyful sound of the waterfall across the lake where I had camped was heard at last. I discovered the little pine thicket in which my nest was, and then I had a rest such as only a mountaineer may enjoy.' In one long day he made his way back across the divide and rejoined his artist friends, to their great relief.

Muir's interest was highly excited by the glaciers he had seen in the Ritter region. Here was a field from which he could learn much. A second visit was inevitable. The following year he wrote to his sister, 'I have just returned from the longest and hardest trip I have ever made in the mountains, having been gone over five weeks.'[23] On this trip, after visiting the Merced peaks, he crossed the divide to the San Joaquin into what he calls the 'slate Yosemite'. He took the Ritter Fork, which 'comes down the mountain here in a network of cascades, wonderfully woven, as are all slate cascades of great size near summits, where the slate has a cleavage well pronounced. The mountains rise in a circle, showing their grand dark bosses and delicate spires on the starry sky.' He pushed on, up to the glaciers of Mount Ritter. He 'thought of ascending the highest Minaret, which is one farthest south, but after scanning it narrowly, discovered it was inaccessible.' Was Muir becoming cautious? He came presently to a glacier with a 'mass of yawning crevasses'. 'It ought not to be set foot upon by solitary explorers, as many of the most dangerous crevasses are slightly snow-covered even this late in the season.' He worked along the margins and found a narrow pass through the Minarets, by which he reached his camp 'after a rich day'. Before leaving the region he scaled two peaks then crossed the familiar divide to the Tuolumne and camped near the Lyell glacier. 'Bread about gone. Home tomorrow or next day.'[24]

Glaciers and their effect upon mountain landscape were not the only objects of John Muir's excursions. Other aspects of nature soon absorbed him even more: living things – birds, flowers, and above all trees. Before quitting the Sierra temporarily for other great primitive areas, notably Alaska, he made three long expeditions southward from Yosemite that laid the foundation for what was his major lifework: the preservation of at least part of our heritage of forest lands and the interpretation of their value as an essential factor in a wholesome national life. These expeditions were of quite different character from his solitary coverage of the Yosemite region. On the first two he was accompanied by others who could both absorb his teachings and assist him in his observations. So, at the end of the summer of 1873, he left the Mariposa Grove bound for the canyons of the San Joaquin in the unwonted posture of riding a horse. With him were Dr Albert Kellogg, botanist, of the California Academy of Sciences, and a young man named Billy Sims, who aimed to be an artist. Galen Clark also came along for the first part of the trip. They crossed the branches of the San Joaquin, descending and climbing vast canyon walls, then went up to the headwaters of the South Fork. There Muir left his companions and his horse and ran (doubtless at times literally) up to the summit peaks. He mentions an ascent of 'Mount Humphreys or the mountain next south',[25] but more important than any mountain was the discovery of a band of wild sheep.

> Eagerly I marked the flowing undulations of their firm, braided muscles, their strong legs, ears, eyes, heads, their graceful rounded necks, the colour of their hair, and the bold upsweeping

curves of their noble horns. Presently they came to a steep, ice-burnished acclivity, which they ascended by a succession of quick, short, stiff-legged leaps, reaching the top without a struggle. This was the most startling feat of mountaineering I had ever witnessed.[26]

He continued to watch their progress with admiration and keen sympathy.

Muir returned to his companions and together they took a lower route across the basin of the North Fork of Kings River, down to the main river and up the south bank to Thomas' Mill. Here they encountered the Sequoias again, and Muir grieved at the vandalism and destruction among them. But a little higher, on the Kings–Kaweah divide, prospects were brighter. 'The Yosemite[27] scenery about the many forks of Kings River presents sublime combinations of cliff and canyon and bossy dome, with high, sharp peaks in the distance.' One black peak with a small snow patch he thought was Mount Goddard. They descended into Kings Canyon, where he found many comparisons with the Merced Yosemite. Leaving Kellogg and Sims with the animals, Muir again set out alone for the high peaks. Snatches from his notebook describe his experiences:

Hard travelling along this portion of the stream, the avalanche material planted with poplars and chaparral–ascended two peaks in the afternoon–the moon is doing marvels in whitening the peaks with a pearly lustre–I have levelled a little spot on the mountainside where I may nap by my fireside–I am blanket-less–set out early for Mount Tyndall and reached the summit about 9 a.m.–descended and pushed back to the main camp–arrived about noon to find Billy and Dr Kellogg gone–pushed on after them, following their trail toward Kearsarge Pass–scenery at the summit is grand–overtook the runaway train at sunset, a mile over the divide–in a few hours passed from ice and snow to the torrid plain.[28]

In Owens Valley, Muir left his two companions again for a ten-day trip to Mount Whitney, and then rejoining them went north through Owens Valley to Lake Tahoe.

Muir's climactic year in the Sierra was in 1875, when he made two memorable trips southward from Yosemite. The first was in July, accompanied by George B Bayley and Charles E Washburn, 'with "Buckskin Bill" as mule master, all well mounted on tough, obstinate mules.'[29] Avoiding the canyons of the San Joaquin, they angled down through the foothills and crossed the Kings at Centerville, almost in the Valley. They climbed up to the forest again and meandered through the Sequoia groves, 'where they heard the sound of axes, and soon came upon a group of busy men engaged in preparing a butt section of a Giant Sequoia they had felled for exhibition at the Quaker Centennial. Many a poor defrauded town dweller will pay his dollar and peep, and gain some dead arithmetical notion of the bigness of our Big Trees, but a true and living knowledge is not to be had at so cheap a rate. As well try to send a section of the storms on which they feed.' They went on and up among the Giant Sequoias to the rim of Kings Canyon, where they noted the close resemblance to Yosemite as seen from Inspiration Point. 'Bayley's joy usually finds expression,' writes Muir, 'in a kind of explosive Indian war whoop, and wild echoes were driven rudely from cliff to cliff, as the varied landscapes revealed themselves from the more commanding points along the trail.' They camped on the river-bank 'near a small circular meadow, that is one of the most perfect flower-gardens I have ever discovered in the mountains. It was filled with lilies and violets, and orchids, and sun-loving golden rods and asters, and ceanothus, with a hundred others all in bloom. Here I lived a fine unmeasured hour "considering the lilies", warming among the mellow waving golden rods and gazing into the countenances of small white violets.' But in all this beauty there was a tragic warning. A sign was posted claiming the land for private ownership. For John Muir it was a signal for beginning a campaign to save these park-like lands for all the people, a campaign that was to dominate his life in the years to come.

The little party kept on up to Kearsarge Pass and down to Owens Valley, whence Muir led them to Mount Whitney ('Buckskin Bill' excepted), an excursion which, as before, needs the explanation given in the next chapter.

The last of Muir's long trips through the Sierra was a solitary one, that is, if we except his 'little Brownie mule'. The purpose of the trip was to learn what he could of the 'peculiar distribution of the Sequoia and its history in general'.[30] From the Mariposa Grove he came to the Fresno Grove, where he met a friendly hermit, relic of the gold-hunting era, named John A Nelder, who helped him find the best examples of Sequoias. In crossing the wide basin of the San Joaquin he took note of the complete absence of Sequoias until he came to Dinkey Creek, a tributary of the Kings. 'Down into the main Kings River canyon, a mile deep, I led and dragged and shoved my patient, much-enduring mule, until in a day and a half we reached old Thomas' mill flat. Thence striking off northeastward I found a magnificent forest. Here five or six days were spent, and it was delightful to learn from countless trees, old and young, how comfortably they were settled down in concordance with climate and soil and their noble neighbours.' Muir was now enjoying one of the supreme experiences of his life. 'Day after day,' he continues, 'from grove to grove, canyon to canyon, I made a long, wavering way, terribly rough in some places for Brownie, but cheery for me, for Big Trees were seldom out of sight. We climbed into the noble forest on the Marble and Middle Fork divide. After a general exploration of the Kaweah basin, this part of the Sequoia belt seemed to me the finest, and I then named it "the Giant Forest".[31]

Here Muir encountered the patriarch settler of the region, Hale Tharp, who had visited the Giant Forest as early as 1858 and for some years had used it as a cattle range. Tharp had adapted a hollow Sequoia log as a cabin and invited Muir to stay with him in what Muir described as 'a spacious log-house of one log, carbon-lined, centuries old, yet sweet and fresh, weather proof, earthquake proof, likely to outlast the most durable stone castle, and commanding views of garden and grove grander far than the richest king ever enjoyed.' But Muir could not linger for long; there was still much to explore. 'There are ways across the Sierra graded by glaciers, well marked, and followed by men and beasts and birds, and one of them even by locomotives; but none natural or artificial along the range. My own ways are easily made in any direction, but Brownie, though one of the toughest and most skilful of his race, was oftentimes discouraged for want of hands, and caused endless work.' Nevertheless, they kept on, 'Sequoias on every ridge-top beckoning and pointing the way'.

Muir encountered a forest fire, which he described in great detail. And then, 'toward sundown two thousand sheep beneath a cloud of dust came streaming through the grand Sequoias.' 'All the basin,' Muir adds, 'was swept by swarms of hoofed locusts.' The southernmost range of the Big Trees was not far away, and Muir pursued them to the end, at the South Fork of Deer Creek and just over a pass to the east side of the Kern River divide.

Muir's biographer, Linnie Marsh Wolfe, sums up: 'From this autumn journey stemmed two important results: a first-hand knowledge of land-and-water monopoly, and a greatly strengthened resolve to lead men back to the healing powers of nature.'[32] From that time on, scientific inquiry, although not by any means extinguished, was dimmed by his devotion to the cause of Conservation.

MUIR'S CLIMBS OF MOUNT WHITNEY
from *History of the Sierra Nevada*

At the end of September 1873 the record of ascents of Mount Whitney stood: (1) August 18: Charles D Begole, Albert H Johnson, John Lucas; (2) late August: William Crapo, Abe Leyda; (3) September 6: William Crapo, William L Hunter, Tom McDonough, Carl Rabe; (4) September 19: Clarence King, Frank Knowles. These ascents were made from the southwest, coming north from the Hockett Trail; King and Knowles from Visalia, the others from Lone Pine by way of Cottonwood Pass.

A new epoch begins with the coming of John Muir in October of that year. When Muir left his companions at the foot of Kearsarge Pass, he rode alone southward along the foot of the range and took the usual route from Lone Pine over Cottonwood Pass. Leaving his horse in a meadow, he climbed the false Mount Whitney and from there saw, as others had done, the higher peak a few miles away. Without delay he ran down, moved his horse to another meadow, and by a very rough way up and down ridges and canyons reached the base of the true Mount Whitney at sunset the same day. As there was no wood for a fire, he made up his mind to spend the night climbing. 'I was among summit needles by midnight or 11 o'clock,' he writes in his diary. 'Had to dance all night to keep from freezing. Was feeble and starving next morning and had to turn back without gaining the top. Was exhausted ere I reached horse and camp and food.' He returned to Independence, ate, and slept all next day; then, not to be defeated, 'set out afoot for the summit by direct course up the east side'. He camped in the sagebrush the first night and next morning made his way up the North Fork of Lone Pine Creek and camped at timber line. On the morning of 21st October, at eight o'clock, he was on the summit of Mount Whitney. There he found Clarence King's record and a memento left by Rabe with a note, 'Notice Gentleman however is the looky finder of this half a Dollar is wellkom to it Carl Rabe Sep 6th 1873.' Muir sketched, gained glorious views, left the half a dollar where he found it, and descended to the foot of the mountain by the way he came. He was back at Independence next day. Many years later Muir wrote, 'For climbers there is a canyon which comes down from the north shoulder of the Whitney peak. Well-seasoned limbs will enjoy the climb of 9000 feet required for this direct route, but soft, succulent people should go the mule way.' Should someone of the present generation of mountain climbers feel inclined to make light of John Muir's exploit, let him endeavour to duplicate it, starting from Independence (not Lone Pine) on foot, with or without sleeping bag and modern concentrated foods – Muir had neither.

Muir's second visit to Mount Whitney came two years later. This time he took his two companions with him to the top. He knew the way and could proceed unerringly. He followed his former route up the North Fork of Lone Pine Creek until he came to the final climb. There he made a variation, crossing the main crest a little to the north, and descended to a lake on the western side. They passed along the rocky shores, 'gradually climbed higher, mounting in a spiral around the northwest shoulder of the mountain, then directly to the summit'. Their arrival was 'duly announced by Bayley as soon as he was rested into a whooping condition.' Undemonstrative Washburn examined the records of antecedent visitors, then remarked with becoming satisfaction, 'I'm the first and only student visitor to visit this highest land in North America.' The descent is described by Muir in one sentence: 'We left the summit about noon and swooped to the torrid plains before sundown, as if dropping out of the sky.'

NOTES AND REFERENCES

1. Muir, 'Studies in the Sierra', *Overland Monthly*, June 1874.
2. Whitney Survey, *The Yosemite Guide-Book*, 1869.
3. Muir, 'Studies in the Sierra', *Overland Monthly*, June 1874. A summary of the conflicting theories is in François E Matthes, 'Geologic History of the Yosemite Valley', U.S. Geological Survey *Professional Paper* 160, 1930; also ME Beatty, 'A Brief Story of the Geology of the Yosemite Valley,' *YNN*, April 1943. The final demolition of Whitney's 'convulsive' theory and the verification of Muir's glacial theory came through a series of seismic explorations conducted by John P Buwalda, Professor of Geology at California Institute of Technology, in 1934–1935, in which it was found that Yosemite was a glacial U-shaped valley far deeper than the present floor of alluvial deposits would indicate. Buwalda, 'Form and Depth of the Bedrock Trough of Yosemite Valley', *YNN*, October 1941; and Beno Gutenberg, John P Buwalda, and Robert P Sharp, 'Seismic Explorations on the Floor of Yosemite Valley, California', *Bulletin of the Geological Society of America*, August 1956.
4. Muir, *First Summer*.
5. Ibid.
6. Ibid.
7. Wolfe, *John of the Mountains*.
8. Badè, *Life and Letters*.
9. Wolfe, *John of the Mountains*.
10. Judge Gilbert W Colby, of Benicia, father of William E Colby, the great Sierra Club leader and disciple of John Muir.
11. For the Yelverton story see her *Zanita, A Tale of the Yosemite*, 1872 (Farquhar No.11), and her *Teresina in America*, 1875; also Charles Warren Stoddard, *In the Footprints of the Padres*, 1902 (the chapter, 'A Mysterious History,' is omitted in the 1911 edition); Mary Viola Lawrence, 'A Summer with a Countess,' *Overland Monthly*, November, 1871; Badè, *Life and Letters*; Wolfe, *Son of the Wilderness*.
12. Joseph LeConte (1823–1901), a native of Georgia, a pupil of Agassiz, was invited to a professorship in the newly founded University of California in Berkeley. 'In the summer of 1870, at the end of the first session of the University, eight of the students invited Professor Frank Soulé, Jr., and me to join them in a camping trip to the Sierras, and we joyfully accepted. This trip was almost an era in my life – perfect health, the merry party of young men, the glorious scenery, and, above all, the magnificent opportunity for studying mountain origin and structure' (*The Autobiography of Joseph LeConte*, edited by William Dallam Armes, 1903). See also LeConte's *A Journal of Ramblings through the High Sierra of California* by the 'University Excursion Party', 1875, and subsequent editions (Farquhar No.14).
13. James Bradley Thayer, *A Western Journey with Emerson*, Boston, 1884; Badè, *Life and Letters*; Muir, *Our National Parks*; Samuel T Farquhar, 'John Muir and Ralph Waldo Emerson', *SCB*, June 1934, 19.3.

14. Muir, 'Explorations in the Great Tuolumne Canyon', *Overland Monthly*, August 1873; reprinted in *SCB*, 1924, 12:1.

15. Muir, 'Living Glaciers of California', *Overland Monthly*, December 1872; also *Harper's New Monthly Magazine*, November 1875.

16. Whitney, 'The Climatic Changes of Later Geologic Times', *in Contributions to American Geology*, vol.II, Cambridge, Mass.: Museum of Comparative Zoology, 1882.

17. Clarence King, *Systematic Geology*, 1878.

18. Israel C Russell, *Glaciers of North America*, 1897; Andrew C Lawson, 'The Sierra Nevada', *University of California Chronicle*, April 1891, 23:2; François E Matthes, 'John Muir and the Glacial Theory of Yosemite', *SCB*, April 1938, 23:9.

19. JM Hutchings, *In the Heart of the Sierras*, 1886.

20. *Letters of John Boies Tileston*, Boston, privately printed, 1922; Mountaineering Notes, *SCB*, 1926, 12.3.

21. Wolfe, *Son of the Wilderness*.

22. Muir, 'In the Heart of the California Alps', *Scribner's*, July 1880; Muir, *Mountains of California*.

23. Badè, *Life and Letters*.

24. Wolfe, *John of the Mountains*. The two peaks may have been Banner and either Davis or Rodgers.

25. Probably not the peak now known as Humphreys; more likely Darwin.

26. Muir, *Mountains of California*.

27. Muir uses 'yosemite' as a generic term for Yosemite-like canyons.

28. Wolfe, *John of the Mountains*. Muir was probably mistaken about the identity of Mount Tyndall; it seems unlikely that even Muir could have reached Mount Tyndall in the time stated.

29. Muir, 'Summering in the Sierra,' *San Francisco Daily Evening Bulletin*, 13 August, 1875; reprinted in *SCB*, 1941, 26:1.

30. The trip in September 1875 is described in Muir, *Our National Parks*.

31. This appears to be the earliest mention of the name 'Giant Forest' (*San Francisco Bulletin*, 22 August, 1875).

32. Wolfe, *Son of the Wilderness*.

3

A SCOTTISH CLIMBER
ON CATHEDRAL PEAK

Ken Crocket

Ken Crocket is a well-known Scottish climber and editor of the
Scottish Mountaineering Club Journal.

On one level, this is the account of my own experience on Cathedral Peak
in Yosemite National Park, first climbed by the Scottish-American
conservationist John Muir in 1869. Over a century after Muir's historic
first ascent, I was able to perch on the same pinnacle. As I rested after a
thrilling climb, the vast gulf of time between myself and Muir was
bridged by the experience of retracing his route and enjoying the
magnificent scenery which he first witnessed from this spot. On another
level, this essay attempts to set Muir's mountaineering achievements in the
context of Scottish and European climbers of the early 19th century. For
clarity of definition, I take the word 'mountaineering' here to mean the
ascent of mountains by routes which are more technically demanding
than hill-walking; such routes will require the frequent use of all four
limbs and will have steep and possibly exposed sections of rock, snow and
ice.

John Muir sailed away from Scotland in 1849, at the age of eleven. He
was born in the North Sea fishing port of Dunbar, thirty miles
southeast of Edinburgh, but could not have found any local role-
model for his future climbing career. The idea of mountaineering as a
recreational pursuit was only just beginning to stir in Scotland; no
mountaineering club was constituted at that period, and the first did
not appear until the 1880s – ten years after Muir's mountain baptism
in the High Sierra of California.[1]

Like any dare-devil boy on that rocky coast, Muir explored the pristine beaches of East Lothian and rambled among the glens of the Lammermuir hills. In his autobiography he describes the grave risks he took climbing upon the crumbling battlements and sea-washed dungeons of Dunbar Castle. These sixty-foot ruins, tottering on their sea-crag foundations, are now considered too dangerous for such scrambling, and public access is officially forbidden.

Muir's wild adventures contrasted sharply with the dry-as-dust lessons he had to endure at school, where learning by rote was enforced with beatings, as was customary. With his pals John Muir savoured the wild songs of the skylark and the mavis (song-thrush), guddled for trout in the rushing burns and waded in the white surf of Belhaven bay. The 1868 journal of his thousand-mile walk to the Gulf of Mexico, records a haunting memory of this boyhood in Scotland. He was hot, dusty and still a day's walk from the Gulf coast, when a salt-laden breeze brought an echo of his childhood ocean.

He wrote:'. . . before I had time to think, a whole flood of long-dormant associations rolled in upon me. The Firth of Forth, the Bass Rock, Dunbar Castle, and the winds and rocks and hills came upon the wings of that wind, and stood in as clear and sudden light as a landscape flashed upon the view by a blaze of lightning in a dark night.'[2]

It is not surprising that he recalled the Bass Rock, a dramatic remnant volcano whose impregnable cliffs soar 400 ft from the sea off North Berwick. It was here, in the late 17th century, that one of the first professional climbers in Scotland earned a crust by catching gannets for the dinner table. Despite their fishy taste, these great seabirds were a delicacy in Scotland throughout Victoria's reign. It is possible that the exploits, and occasional deaths of the gannet-hunters on these treacherous cliffs would have been known to the Muir family, since the Bass dominates Dunbar's seascape. John Muir explored the rocky beaches and cliffs of his parish, acquiring skills for scrambling and balancing on sea-shore boulders, which would be of great value in later years. Such childhood scrambles are often the spur to later adventures. But what was happening in the Scottish hills during the mid-19th century?

The Gaiter Club was founded in 1849 with the genteel aim of 'encouraging its members to enjoy beautiful scenery'. And although the club members did not chalk-up any noted ascents, some later helped to found the Scottish Mountaineering Club; indeed Professor Ramsay, became the SMC's first president.

The Gaiter Club was followed in 1866 by the Cobbler Club, named for the peak at the head of Loch Long, whose members 'stravaiged' widely 'from Tinto to Ben Lomond and from Dumyat to Dumgoyne.'[3]

So it is unlikely that John Muir would have been exposed to any developed culture of mountaineering before he left Scotland in 1849. The rare individuals who had climbed any Scottish summits at that period were usually hunting minerals, semi-precious stones or rare plants, though survey parties had also climbed to measure the heights of the hills. But what Muir clearly possessed from early age was a love of adventure and the outdoors, matched with an indomitable spirit and a courageous heart. And as the history of climbing reveals, such factors often produce a great mountaineer.

In the summer of 1869, John Muir got his first chance to visit the High Sierra, the year following his arrival in San Francisco at the age of thirty-one. He seems to have been desperate to explore the mountains and after enduring a mountain shepherd's life for one summer, he broke free to explore Yosemite. As *My First Summer in the Sierra* relates, he escaped into the mountains with joyful enthusiasm.[4]

By early September 1869, Muir was planning 'one more good wild excursion among the high peaks, and surely none . . . ever felt so gloriously happily excited by the outlook.'[5] Summer was receding from Yosemite Valley, and by the middle of the month the winter snows would make travel impossible. Indeed, returning from his first ascent of Cathedral Peak, he lost his footing on steep snow and ice and only just stopped short of a deep crevasse by digging his heels into the surface of the slope. Evidently crampons were unknown to him at this time.

For some months he had set his heart on climbing Cathedral Peak. He wrote: 'From the top of the divide, and also from the big Tuolumne Meadows, the wonderful mountain called Cathedral Peak is in sight. From every point of view it shows marked individuality. It is a majestic temple of one stone, hewn from the living rock, and adorned with spires and pinnacles in regular cathedral style.'[6]

On his explorations, Muir took only the bare necessities and indeed often referred to himself as a 'wilderness tramp'; he carried nothing but his everyday clothing, a notebook and some bread, baked rock-hard for the trip. And though he had never received any mountain training, he intuitively grasped potential difficulties before he got into trouble on steep, rocky ground. As a self-taught geologist, he soon developed an expert eye for rock features and could route-find as well as any trained Alpinist of the day.

Muir's geological field-sketches and hand-drawn maps of his explorations are far in advance of any normal amateur of the day. He soon realised that the vast trench of Yosemite Valley could not have been created by the cataclysms and earthquake faults of orthodox geological theory. His first-hand observations revealed that the valley had been shaped by the slow, inexorable erosion of glaciers and rivers exerted over eons of time. Muir's glacial theory posed a challenge to the great Josiah Whitney, the official State Geologist of California, who dismissed the 'sheep-herder's theories' with contempt; but subsequent research confirmed Muir's hypothesis. His *Studies in the Sierra*, which describe the physical forces of mountain building and erosion in great detail, is well worth the attention of any climber with even a passing interest in the rocks beneath his feet.

But what was the expert Alpinist in Scotland and Europe doing at this time?

One of the finest mountain areas in Scotland is the Black Cuillin Ridge of Skye, famed for the superb friction of its gabbro rock and razor-sharp pinnacles; this area was just beginning to be explored and developed as a climbing arena. The eminent scientist Professor James Forbes had climbed Sgurr nan Gillean in 1836 with a local man Duncan Macintyre.

Forbes was admittedly an exceptional pioneer, at a time when the Isle of Skye was considered extremely remote. It was not until 1870, when the mainland railway reached Strome with its ferry link to Portree on Skye, that more climbers were able to visit, and attempts on the island peaks became more common.

But even before John Muir began to explore the Sierra, there were similar pioneers in Scotland, notably Alexander Nicolson, a Skye man who had gone south to England but eventually returned to become a sheriff in Scotland. A noted Gaelic scholar, he declined the offer of a chair in Gaelic Studies at the University of Edinburgh. In 1865, he retraced Forbes' climb of Sgurr nan Gillean (known today as 'the Tourist Route'), with MacIntyre, the innkeeper from Sligachan whose father had climbed with Forbes in 1836. They descended by a new route, known thereafter as 'Nicolson's Chimney'.

On his expeditions in the Cuillin, Nicolson wore a tartan plaid, the traditional wool blanket used by the Scottish Highlander for every purpose, including bivouacs on the mountain. In an emergency, the plaid could even be used as a short rope for traversing minor obstacles. Nicolson also made the first ascent of Sgurr Alasdair on the Cuillin ridge in 1873 and the peak was named in his honour. He later returned to live in Edinburgh, where he died in January 1893, aged 66. (Coincidentally, in the summer of that same year John Muir came to Scotland for his only return visit, when he travelled throughout the Highlands.)

In 1857, some eight years before the historic ascent of Sgurr Alasdair, the famous Alpine Club was formed in London, 'for the promotion of good fellowship among mountaineers, of mountain climbing and exploration throughout the world, and of better knowledge of the mountains through literature, science and art'. The classic Alpine peaks had been under sustained attack since the first ascent of Mont Blanc in 1786. For the next four decades or so almost all alpine ascents invariably had a scientific purpose in mind: could a human breathe at such high altitudes? At what temperature did water boil at various heights? What was the precise shade of blue of the sky beyond the summits?

The first American ascent of Mont Blanc was made in 1819 by Howard and Van Rensselaer, two graduates visiting centres of medical excellence in Europe. In 1815, the Treaty of Vienna had opened Europe to a flood of tourists and travellers. The doctors' ascent of Mont Blanc was made with the typical brio and refreshing style of New World climbers; it appeared that scientific discovery was not the only reason for climbing peaks: curiosity, physical challenge and vigorous exercise were equally valid motives, and 'peak-bagging' also came into it.

Commercialisation entered the European arena as early as 1823, when the Chamonix Corporation was set up to regulate the mountain guide profession. The agency also ensured that the flow of income from climbing tourists would continue to enrich the district. This highlighted one of the major differences between mountaineering in Britain and mountaineering in the Alps; in Europe guides were automatically engaged by climbing-parties, whereas in Britain very few guides existed. One notable exception, however, was John Mackenzie of Skye, who forged a long-lasting and productive partnership with Norman Collie. However it is probably true to say that in their climbing relationship they were not so much 'guide' and 'client' as equal partners.

It is interesting that in Europe at this time ropes were carried, but more for reassurance than real protection. Rope technique improved only slowly through the latter half of the 19th century, and was as much due to amateurs as the professional guides. In the Alps ladders might be carried to bridge glaciers, while for snow and ice work the metal-tipped staff known as the alpenstock gradually gave way to the long, cumbersome ice axe. In 1865, competition for the first ascent of the big, unclimbed summits in the Alps culminated in disaster on the Matterhorn, when four climbers were killed descending after a successful climb. Edward Whymper, one of the survivors, published his classic *Scrambles Amongst the Alps*, in 1871 and it soon adorned John Muir's bookshelf.[7]

Muir however, was more interested in the geology of Yosemite and eagerly accepted delivery of John Tyndall's latest book *The Glaciers of the Alps* in 1871. Tyndall (1820–93) a physicist and author, was considered a competitor for the first ascent of the Matterhorn. He began exploring the mountains for scientific reasons, but gradually put away his notebooks and climbed more often for sheer pleasure. It was also at the end of this year that Muir completed his article 'Yosemite Glaciers', this being the first published hypothesis to propose glaciers as the shapers of Yosemite's topography.

Earlier in 1871, at the beginning of November, Muir made a trip to Hetch Hetchy, the 'Tuolumne Yosemite' as he aptly called it. It was a late fall excursion before snow blanketed Yosemite. His description of this trip succinctly captures his style of exploration:

I went alone, my outfit consisting of a pair of blankets and a quantity of bread and coffee . . . Sunset found me only three miles back from the brow of El Capitan, near the head of a round smooth gap – the deepest groove in the El Capitan ridge. Here I lay down and thought of the time when the groove in which I rested was being ground away at the bottom of a vast ice sheet that flowed over the Sierra like a slow wind . . . My huge camp fire glowed like a sun . . . A happy brook sang confidingly, and by its side I made my bed of rich, spicy boughs, elastic and warm.[8]

Immediately after this exploratory season of 1871 Muir began to publish a series of historic articles which opened eyes and minds in American society. He produced a wealth of informative and entertaining conservation literature influenced by his early education, largely based on the classic King James Version of the Bible, his wide reading and his undoubted powers of observation. In particular, his articles for *Century Magazine* catalysed the national consciousness, leading to the formation of the Sierra Club in 1892, with Muir serving as Founder-President until his death in 1914.

If there is any clue to Muir's innermost thoughts about his solo-climbing exploits, it may be read in a letter to his mother, written in November 1871, when his explorations for that year had been halted by snow. As the following extract indicates, he was on the brink of his writing career: 'I have been sleeping in the rocks and snow, often weary and hungry, sustained by the excitements of my subject and by the Scottish pluck and perseverance which belongs to our family . . . In all my lonely journeys among the most distant and difficult pathless, passless mountains, I never wander, am never lost. Providence guides through every danger and takes me to all the truths which I need to learn, and some day I hope to show you my sheaves, my big bound pages of mountain gospel.'

His mountaineering was a part of his rich life of exploration, and a part he took in his stride with the minimum of fuss. The summits he trod merely provided him with a better view of his earthly paradise. But the legacy of books, writings and conservation achievements, which Muir bequeathed us, has ensured the survival of this mountain paradise for anyone to enjoy to this day.

. . . The female black bear eyed me suspiciously as I crept closer with my camera. Her two cubs clung to the top of a nearby tree, which they had climbed in an impressively short time upon hearing our voices. Ten minutes ago, I had been warm and snug in my sleeping bag, insulated from the cool night air at 8000 feet in the Californian Sierra. Then my wife had hurriedly announced the bears' nightly visit to the campsite, of which we were the first line of defence. In the High Sierra, black bears rule supreme, but Muir had to contend with the infinitely more menacing presence of wild grizzlies, which sadly were exterminated from California in the early 1900s.

We were camping high in Yosemite National Park, at the edge of Tuolumne's alpine meadows, having left the crowded valley with a mixture of relief and regret. Here, at 4000 feet above the valley it was cooler; and although it was mid-August tourist season, it was much quieter. Before us stretched the meadows, now released from their perennial blanket of snow; a green carpet of alpine flowers and mineral springs, where deer graze and dragonflies enact a glittering aerial ballet.

Behind our campsite the hillside rose steadily towards the Yosemite watershed and stately Cathedral Peak (10,940 feet), our goal for the next day's climb. This was first climbed in 1869 by the Scottish-American conservationist John Muir, who was impressed by the beauty of the peak and its surroundings. Muir had taken an easier approach via the North Face but Colin and I intended to climb Cathedral Peak by its southeast ridge, a classic buttress climb, graded 5.4 in the Yosemite system.

Our trail to Cathedral Peak started from the road bordering Tuolumne Meadows. At first we passed through tall pines, climbing over, under and even through the occasional fallen tree, which the Park Service leaves untouched to enrich the natural habitat. After an hour or so the trees began to thin and broad slabs of glacier-polished granite appeared. These made delightful walking, as the slope rose at a gentle angle. Spring had been late and the hills were spangled with alpine flowers; wherever a rock hollow held sufficient soil, flowers

46

erupted in brilliant yellows, pinks, reds, whites and purples. The fiery-red of Indian Paintbrush, one of my favourites, actually derives from the leaves; the flower itself being small, insignificant and off-white. Lingering in the woods, I recalled John Muir's words describing his first ascent of Cathedral Peak: 'I made my way up to its topmost spire, which I reached at noon, having loitered by the way to study the fine trees.'

As we left the tree line the full glory of the rocky watershed became apparent as it curved from the distinctive spire of Unicorn Peak on the left, along to Echo ridge and the Echo peaks, dropping to a broad pass before soaring abruptly to Cathedral Peak. To the left, nestled beneath the ridge was picturesque Budd Lake, to whose shores we made a short detour; but this paradise was plagued with mosquitoes, and in minutes we were forced to retreat and seek the breezes of the high ridge. We found mysterious patches of pink snow in shady hollows and racked our brains for an explanation of this phenomenon. Was this ash from a recent volcanic eruption in Mexico? Or wind-blown pollen grains? We later learned that this 'water melon snow' is produced by a red algae which grows among the frozen snow crystals. We traversed the highest of these pink-tinged snow-fields to the glacier-smoothed pass with its magnificent views of the Yosemite basin. Only a few wind-tortured trees survive up here, stunted and sculpted by the winter gales. I will never forget one sun-bleached skeleton which stood out against the spectacular backdrop of a dark blue Sierra sky. Looking north along the pass and up towards Cathedral Peak, our chosen route, the southeast ridge, formed the right hand skyline while a prominent finger of rock – the Eichorn Pinnacle – was etched against the sky on the left. The south face proper consists of a series of steep, smooth granite walls, broken only by faint lines of weakness; this evidently provided challenging routes. These granite walls rise to a broken recess high on the face, above which we could see the summit rocks.

We scrambled up loose scree through stunted trees then traversed to the right beneath the south face to arrive at the foot of the climb. Dropping our sacks in the shade of a tree we turned to examine the rocks, only to find ourselves being scrutinised by a fat marmot, basking in the sun. He was perched some twenty feet up the route, but when we attempted a photograph he heaved his bulk off the hot spot and scuffled off behind a flake of rock. Reappearing higher up the slope, he gave a last glare at the intruders and vanished among the rocky mazes of the talus.

Having won first lead on the toss of a coin I stepped gingerly out onto the warm granite. The rock was studded with knuckle-sized crystals of pink feldspar projecting from the softer, eroded rock matrix. When these nobbles are sufficiently large they are called 'chickenheads' and often provide the only holds on an otherwise smooth face. To begin with I was unsure whether I could trust these crystals to bear my full weight, but a spell of uncertain hopping about on a small bulge stimulated the necessary adrenaline, and as our confidence on this unfamiliar rock grew, the climbing soon became enjoyable.

The lower pitches consisted of vertical flutings and granite ribs of various sizes; thin rock flakes offered magnificent pinch holds, while the rounded ribs required us to bridge and jam our way upward. The buttress steepened halfway up and we had to find our route across sheer walls, up vertical cracks and chimneys, hugging close to the rock whenever the westerly breeze increased. Scottish climbers are used to climbing in freezing rain and bitter wind, and normally I would be insulated by layers of waterproof clothing. It was almost surreal to be climbing pitch after pitch of dry rock, in full sunshine, beneath an immense blue sky and wearing just shirts and shorts. A safe belay allowed us to relax and enjoy this climbing heaven, leaning back with closed eyes, to feel the sun warm us to the bones.

As we ascended the mountain, the distant horizon grew wider and more curved, blending with the sky in the thin blue haze of infinity. Perched high on the buttress we traversed left beneath a desperately smooth wall to enter a system of shallow grooves. These provided perhaps the hardest climbing of the day with several moves almost at V.S. grade. I shuddered at the thought of being caught at this spot during a cloudburst, however unlikely that was at present. One move remains engraved on my mind, from when I traversed left across a wall to stand on a chickenhead. The exposure was impressive, looking down the south face and beyond to the trees, curiously foreshortened from this viewpoint. The breeze suddenly came on strong, forcing me to hug the rockface until the wind dropped, when I was able to pull up onto safer holds

Eventually, we sensed that we were approaching the summit, as Colin pulled over a block to gain a series of ledges just below the top. I followed him with a brief hand-traverse right to land in the crack which splits the pinnacle block and mantel-shelved gingerly onto the tiny summit. There was barely space for both of us on top of the peak, and we belayed securely before turning to enjoy the glorious panorama which surrounded us. To the east and north rose the granite domes of Tuolumne Meadows, a famous playground for climbers and mountaineers. To the southeast the far horizon was pierced by the jagged line of the Palisades, while to the west and south lay the more familiar Yosemite peaks. To the south we could see a classic ridge, the Matthes Crest; definitely one to be reserved for a future expedition. On the summit of Cathedral Peak we found a metal case containing an ascent book and were interested to find that several British parties had inscribed their names.

We duly added ourselves to the list and as we sat there and drank it all in we felt a rush of gratitude for John Muir, who made the first ascent of Cathedral Peak, alone, without ropes and without companions. He was a man at one with Nature, and a pioneer climber, well ahead of his time. Without his writings and his long campaigns to protect the natural beauty of such areas as the Yosemite Valley, the conservation movement would have been much poorer; and days such as this would be rare indeed.

NOTES AND REFERENCES

1. I have not touched on the 'Highland Mountain Club of Lochgoilhead', founded in 1815, as this was set up in order to enjoy an annual festival at the summer solstice, the first night of which was spent on the summit of some lofty mountain with much wining, dining and speech-making!

2. William Frederic Badè, *The Life and Letters of John Muir*, Chapter 1, 'The Ancestral Background', p.31. (1924; republished by Bâton Wicks, 1996 as *John Muir, His Life and Letters and Other Writings*).

3. *Scottish Mountaineering Club Journal* 1945, Vol. 23, No. 136, p. 254.

4. John Muir, *My First Summer in the Sierra* (Diadem & The Mountaineers 1992).

5. Ibid., p.281.

6. Ibid., p.263.
7. Edward Whymper, *Scrambles Amongst the Alps in the Years 1860–69* (John Murray, London 1871).
8. Badè, *The Life and Letters of John Muir*, p.158.

4

THE TUOLUMNE CAMP

John Muir

This is an extract from Muir's autobiographical *My First Summer in the Sierra, published in* 1911, derived from the journals of his 1869 Sierra experiences.

August 22. Clouds none, cool west wind, slight hoar-frost on the meadows. Carlo [the dog] is missing; have been seeking him all day. In the thick woods between camp and the river, among tall grass and fallen pines, I discovered a baby fawn. At first it seemed inclined to come to me; but when I tried to catch it, and got within a rod or two, it turned and walked softly away, choosing its steps like a cautious, stealthy, hunting cat. Then, as if suddenly called or alarmed, it began to buck and run like a grown deer, jumping high above the fallen trunks, and was soon out of sight. Possibly its mother may have called it, but I did not hear her. I don't think fawns ever leave the home thicket or follow their mothers until they are called or frightened. I am distressed about Carlo. There are several other camps and dogs not many miles from here, and I still hope to find him. He never left me before. Panthers are very rare here, and I don't think any of these cats would dare touch him. He knows bears too well to be caught by them, and as for Indians, they don't want him.

August 23. Cool, bright day, hinting Indian summer. Mr Delaney has gone to the Smith Ranch, on the Tuolumne below Hetch-Hetchy Valley, thirty-five or forty miles from here, so I'll be alone for a week or more, – not really alone, for Carlo has come back. He was at a camp a few miles to the northwestward. He looked sheepish and ashamed when I asked him where he had been and why he had gone away without leave. He is now trying to get me to caress him and show signs of forgiveness. A wondrous wise dog. A great load is off my mind. I could not have left the mountains without him. He seems very glad to get back to me.

Rose and crimson sunset, and soon after the stars appeared the moon rose in most impressive majesty over the top of Mount Dana. I sauntered up the meadow in the white light. The jet-black shadows were so wonderfully distinct and substantial looking, I often stepped high in crossing them, taking them for black charred logs.

August 24. Another charming day, warm and calm soon after sunrise, clouds only about one percent, – faint, silky cirrus wisps, scarcely visible. Slight frost, Indian summerish, the mountains growing softer in outline and dreamy looking, their rough angles melted off, apparently. Sky at evening with fine, dark, subdued purple, almost like the evening purple of the San Joaquin plains in settled weather. The moon is now gazing over the summit of Dana. Glorious exhilarating air. I wonder if in all the world there is another mountain range of equal height blessed with weather so fine, and so openly kind and hospitable and approachable.

August 25. Cool as usual in the morning, quickly changing to the ordinary serene generous warmth and brightness. Toward evening the west wind was cool and sent us to the campfire. Of all Nature's flowery carpeted mountain halls none can be finer than this glacier meadow. Bees and butterflies seem as abundant as ever. The birds are still here, showing no sign of leaving for winter quarters though the frost must bring them to mind. For my part I should like to stay here all winter or all my life or even all eternity.

August 26. Frost this morning; all the meadow grass and some of the pine needles sparkling with irised crystals, – flowers of light. Large picturesque clouds, craggy like rocks, are piled on Mount Dana, reddish in colour like the mountain itself; the sky for a few degrees around the horizon is pale purple, into which the pines dip their spires with fine effect. Spent the day as usual looking about me, watching the changing lights, the ripening autumn colours of the grass, seeds, late-blooming gentians, asters, goldenrods; parting the meadow grass here and there and looking down into the underworld of mosses and liverworts; watching the busy ants and beetles and other small people at work and play like squirrels and bears in a forest; studying the formation of lakes and meadows, moraines, mountain sculpture; making small beginnings in these directions, charmed by the serene beauty of everything.

The day has been extra cloudy, though bright on the whole, for the clouds were brighter than common. Clouds about 15 percent, which in Switzerland would be considered extra clear. Probably more free sunshine falls on this majestic range than on any other in the world I've ever seen or heard of. It has the brightest weather, brightest glacier-polished rocks, the greatest abundance of irised spray from its glorious waterfalls, the brightest forests of silver firs and silver pines, more star-shine, moonshine, and perhaps more crystal-shine than any other mountain chain, and its countless mirror lakes, having more light poured into them, glow and spangle most. And how glorious the shining after the short summer showers and after frosty nights when the morning sunbeams are pouring through the crystals on the grass and pine needles, and how ineffably spiritually fine is the morning-glow on the mountain-tops and the alpenglow of evening. Well may the Sierra be named, not the Snowy Range, but the Range of Light.

August 27. Clouds only five percent, – mostly white and pink cumuli over the Hoffman spur towards evening, – frosty morning. Crystals grow in marvellous beauty and perfection of form these still nights, every one built as carefully as the grandest holiest temple, as if planned to endure forever.

Contemplating the lace-like fabric of streams outspread over the mountains, we are reminded that everything is flowing – going somewhere, animals and so-called lifeless rocks as well as water. Thus the snow flows fast or slow in grand beauty-making glaciers and avalanches; the air in majestic floods carrying minerals, plant leaves, seeds, spores, with streams of music and fragrance; water streams carrying rocks both in solution, and in the form of mud particles, sand, pebbles, and boulders. Rocks flow from volcanoes like water from springs, and animals flock together and flow in currents modified by stepping, leaping, gliding, flying, swimming, etc. While the stars go streaming through space pulsed on and on forever like blood globules in Nature's warm heart.

August 28. The dawn a glorious song of colour. Sky absolutely cloudless. A fine crop of hoar-frost. Warm after ten o'clock. The gentians don't mind the first frost though their petals seem so delicate; they close every night as if going to sleep, and awake fresh as ever in the morning sun-glory. The grass is a shade browner since last week, but there are no nipped wilted plants of any sort as far as I have seen. Butterflies and the grand host of smaller flies are benumbed every night, but they hover and dance in the sunbeams over the meadows before noon with no apparent lack of playful, joyful life. Soon they must all fall like petals in an orchard, dry and wrinkled, not a wing of all the mighty host left to tingle the air. Nevertheless new myriads will arise in the spring, rejoicing, exulting, as if laughing cold death to scorn.

August 29. Clouds about five percent, slight frost. Bland serene Indian summer weather. Have been gazing all day at the mountains, watching the changing lights. More and more plainly are they clothed with light as a garment, white tinged with pale purple, palest during the midday hours, richest in the morning and evening. Everything seems consciously peaceful, thoughtful, faithfully waiting God's will.

August 30. This day just like yesterday. A few clouds motionless and apparently with no work to do beyond looking beautiful. Frost enough for crystal building, – glorious fields of ice-diamonds destined to last but a night. How lavish is Nature building, pulling down, creating, destroying, chasing every material particle from form to form, ever changing, ever beautiful.

Mr Delaney arrived this morning. Felt not a trace of loneliness while he was gone. On the contrary, I never enjoyed grander company. The whole wilderness seems to be alive and familiar, full of humanity. The very stones seem talkative, sympathetic, brotherly. No wonder when we consider that we all have the same Father and Mother.

August 31. Clouds five percent. Silky cirrus wisps and fringes so fine they almost escape notice. Frost enough for another crop of crystals

Previous Page: Half Dome, originally called South Dome
Above Photograph: Yosemite Valley with Bridalveil Fall on the right
(photos courtesy of Graham White)

Main Photograph: Mt Ritter from Lake Catherine, showing the route of Muir's first ascent

Opposite Inset: South-east glacier of Mt Ritter, looking towards The Minarets and High Sierra Crest

Above Inset: Mt Lyell from Mt McClure, with Banner Peak and Mount Ritter beyond *(photos courtesy of Dr Terry Isles)*

Top Photograph: Cathedral Peak
(photo courtesy of Ken Crocket)

Bottom Photograph: The Minarets from the John Muir Trail
(photo courtesy of Graham White)

Opposite Page: Cathedral Peak
(photo courtesy of Ken Crocket)

Top Photograph: Mt Whitney from summit of Mt Barnard
Bottom Photograph: Mt Langley from summit of Mt Whitney
(photos courtesy of Nigel Hawkins)

on the meadows but none on the forests. The gentians, goldenrods, asters, etc., don't seem to feel it; neither petals nor leaves are touched though they seem so tender. Every day opens and closes like a flower, noiseless, effortless. Divine peace glows on all the majestic landscape like the silent enthusiastic joy that sometimes transfigures a noble human face.

September 1. Clouds five percent – motionless, of no particular colour – ornaments with no hint of rain or snow in them. Day all calm – another grand throb of Nature's heart, ripening late flowers and seeds for next summer, full of life and the thoughts and plans of life to come, and full of ripe and ready death beautiful as life, telling divine wisdom and goodness and immortality. Have been up Mount Dana, making haste to see as much as I can now that the time of departure is drawing nigh. The views from the summit reach far and wide, eastward over the Mono Lake and Desert; mountains beyond mountains looking strangely barren and grey and bare like heaps of ashes dumped from the sky. The lake, eight or ten miles in diameter, shines like a burnished disk of silver, no trees about its grey, ashy, cindery shores. Looking westward, the glorious forests are seen sweeping over countless ridges and hills, girdling domes and subordinate mountains, fringing in long curving lines the dividing ridges, and filling every hollow where the glaciers have spread soil-beds however rocky or smooth. Looking northward and southward along the axis of the range, you see the glorious array of high mountains, crags and peaks and snow, the fountain-heads of rivers that are flowing west to the sea through the famous Golden Gate, and east to hot salt lakes and deserts to evaporate and hurry back into the sky. Innumerable lakes are shining like eyes beneath heavy rock brows, bare or tree fringed, or imbedded in black forests. Meadow openings in the woods seem as numerous as the lakes or perhaps more so. Far up the moraine-covered slopes and among crumbling rocks I found many delicate hardy plants, some of them still in flower. The best gains of this trip were the lessons of unity and interrelation of all the features of the landscape revealed in general views. The lakes and meadows are located just where the ancient glaciers bore heaviest at the foot of the steepest parts of their channels, and of course their longest diameters are approximately parallel with each other and with the belts of forests growing in long curving lines on the lateral and medial moraines, and in broad outspreading fields on the terminal beds deposited toward the end of the ice period when the glaciers were receding. The domes, ridges, and spurs also show the influence of glacial action in their forms, which approximately seem to be the forms of greatest strength with reference to the stress of over sweeping, past-sweeping, down-grinding ice-streams; survivals of the most resisting masses, or those most favourably situated. How interesting everything is! Every rock, mountain, stream, plant, lake, lawn, forest, garden, bird, beast, insect seems to call and invite us to come and learn something of its history and relationship. But shall the poor ignorant scholar be allowed to try the lessons they offer? It seems too great and good to be true. Soon I'll be going to the lowlands. The bread camp must soon be removed. If I had a few sacks of flour, an axe, and some matches, I would build a cabin of pine logs, pile up plenty of firewood about it and stay all winter to see the grand fertile snowstorms, watch the birds and animals that winter thus high, how they live, how the forests look snow-laden or buried, and how the avalanches look and sound on their way down the mountains. But now I'll have to go, for there is nothing to spare in the way of provisions. I'll surely be back, however, surely I'll be back. No other place has ever so overwhelmingly attracted me as this hospitable, Godful wilderness.

September 2. A grand, red, rosy, crimson day, – a perfect glory of a day. What it means I don't know. It is the first marked change from tranquil sunshine with purple mornings and evenings and still, white moons. There is nothing like a storm, however. The average cloudiness only about eight percent, and there is no sighing in the woods to betoken a big weather change. The sky was red in the morning and evening, the colour not diffused like the ordinary purple glow, but loaded upon separate well-defined clouds that remained motionless, as if anchored around the jagged mountain-fenced horizon. A deep-red cap, bluffy around its sides, lingered a long time on Mount Dana and Mount Gibbs, drooping so low as to hide most of their bases, but leaving Dana's round summit free, which seemed to float separate and alone over the big crimson cloud. Mammoth Mountain, to the south of Gibbs and Bloody Canyon, striped and spotted with snow-banks and clumps of dwarf pine, was also favoured with a glorious crimson cap, in the making of which there was no trace of economy – a huge bossy pile coloured with a perfect passion of crimson that seemed important enough to be sent off to burn among the stars in majestic independence. One is constantly reminded of the infinite lavishness and fertility of Nature – inexhaustible abundance amid what seems enormous waste. And yet when we look into any of her operations that lie within reach of our minds, we learn that no particle of her material is wasted or worn out. It is eternally flowing from use to use, beauty to yet higher beauty; and we soon cease to lament waste and death, and rather rejoice and exult in the imperishable, unspendable wealth of the universe, and faithfully watch and wait the reappearance of everything that melts and fades and dies about us, feeling sure that its next appearance will be better and more beautiful than the last.

I watched the growth of these red-lands of the sky as eagerly as if new mountain ranges were being built. Soon the group of snowy peaks in whose recesses lie the highest fountains of the Tuolumne, Merced, and North Fork of the San Joaquin were decorated with majestic coloured clouds like those already described, but more complicated, to correspond with the grand fountain-heads of the rivers they overshadowed. The Sierra Cathedral, to the south of camp, was overshadowed like Sinai. Never before noticed so fine a union of rock and cloud in form and colour and substance, drawing earth and sky together as one; and so human is it, every feature and tint of colour goes to one's heart, and we shout, exulting in wild enthusiasm as if all the divine show were our own. More and more, in a place like this, we feel ourselves part of wild Nature, kin to everything. Spent most of the day high up on the north rim of the valley, commanding views of the clouds in all their red glory spreading their wonderful light over all the basin, while the rocks and trees and small Alpine plants at my feet seemed hushed and thoughtful, as if they also were conscious spectators of the glorious new cloud-world.

Here and there, as I plodded farther and higher, I came to small garden-patches and ferneries just where one would naturally decide that no plant-creature could possibly live. But, as in the region about the head of Mono Pass and the top of Dana, it was in the wildest, highest places that the most beautiful and tender and enthusiastic plant-people were found. Again and again, as I lingered over these charming plants, I said, How came you here? How do you live through the winter? Our roots, they explained, reach far down the joints of the summer-warmed rocks, and beneath our fine snow mantle killing frosts cannot reach us, while we sleep away the dark half of the year dreaming of spring.

Ever since I was allowed entrance into these mountains I have been looking for cassiope, said to be the most beautiful and best loved of the heathworts, but, strange to say, I have not yet found it. On my high mountain walks I keep muttering, 'Cassiope, cassiope'. This name, as Calvinists say, is driven in upon me, notwithstanding the glorious host of plants that come about me uncalled as soon as I show myself. Cassiope seems the highest name of all the small mountain-heath people, and as if conscious of her worth, keeps out of my way. I must find her soon, if at all this year.

September 4. All the vast sky dome is clear, filled only with mellow Indian summer light. The pine and hemlock and fir cones are nearly ripe and are falling fast from morning to night, cut off and gathered by the busy squirrels. Almost all the plants have matured their seeds, their summer work done; and the summer crop of birds and deer will soon be able to follow their parents to the foothills and plains at the approach of winter, when the snow begins to fly.

September 5. No clouds. Weather cool, calm, bright as if no great thing were yet ready to be done. Have been sketching the North Tuolumne Church. The sunset gloriously coloured.

September 6. Still another perfectly cloudless day, purple evening and morning, all the middle hours one mass of pure serene sunshine. Soon after sunrise the air grew warm, and there was no wind. One naturally halted to see what Nature intended to do. There is a suggestion of real Indian summer in the hushed brooding, faintly hazy weather. The yellow atmosphere, though thin, is still plainly of the same general character as that of eastern Indian summer. The peculiar mellowness is perhaps in part caused by myriad of ripe spores adrift in the sky.

Mr Delaney now keeps up a solemn talk about the need of getting away from these high mountains, telling sad stories of flocks that perished in storms that broke suddenly into the midst of fine innocent weather like this we are now enjoying. 'In no case,' said he, 'will I venture to stay so high and far back in the mountains as we now are later than the middle of this month, no matter how warm and sunny it may be.' He would move the flock slowly at first, a few miles a day until the Yosemite Creek basin was reached and crossed, then while lingering in the heavy pine woods should the weather threaten he could hurry down to the foothills, where the snow never falls deep enough to smother a sheep. Of course I am anxious to see as much of the wilderness as possible in the few days left me, and I say again, – May the good time come when I can stay as long as I like with plenty of bread, far and free from trampling flocks, though I may well be thankful for this generous foodful inspiring summer. Anyhow we never know where we must go nor what guides we are to get, – men, storms, guardian angels, or sheep. Perhaps almost everybody in the least natural is guarded more than he is ever aware of. All the wilderness seems to be full of tricks and plans to drive and draw us up into God's Light.

Have been busy planning, and baking bread for at least one more good wild excursion among the high peaks, and surely none, however hopefully aiming at fortune or fame, ever felt so gloriously happily excited by the outlook.

September 7. Left camp at daybreak and made direct for Cathedral Peak, intending to strike eastward and southward from that point among the peaks and ridges at the heads of the Tuolumne, Merced, and San Joaquin Rivers. Down through the pine woods I made my way, across the Tuolumne River and meadows, and up the heavily timbered slope forming the south boundary of the upper Tuolumne basin, along the east side of Cathedral Peak, and up to its topmost spire, which I reached at noon, having loitered by the way to study the fine trees – two-leaved pine, mountain pine, albicaulis pine, silver fir, and the most charming, most graceful of all the evergreens, the mountain hemlock. High, cool, late-flowering meadows also detained me, and lakelets and avalanche tracks and huge quarries of moraine rocks above the forests.

All the way up from the Big Meadows to the base of the Cathedral the ground is covered with moraine material, the left lateral moraine of the great glacier that must have completely filled this upper Tuolumne basin. Higher there are several small terminal moraines of residual glaciers shoved forward at right angles against the grand simple lateral of the main Tuolumne Glacier. A fine place to study mountain sculpture and soil-making. The view from the Cathedral Spires is very fine and telling in every direction. Innumerable peaks, ridges, domes, meadows, lakes, and woods; the forests extending in long curving lines and broad fields wherever the glaciers have left soil for them to grow on, while the sides of the highest mountains show a straggling dwarf growth clinging to rifts in the rocks apparently independent of soil. The dark heath-like growth on the Cathedral roof I found to be dwarf snow-pressed albicaulis pine, about three or four feet high, but very old looking. Many of them are bearing cones, and the noisy Clarke crow is eating the seeds, using his long bill like a woodpecker in digging them out of the cones. A good many flowers are still in bloom about the base of the peak, and even on the roof among the little pines, especially a woody yellow-flowered eriogonum and a handsome aster. The body of the Cathedral is nearly square, and the roof slopes are wonderfully regular and symmetrical, the ridge trending northeast and southwest. This direction has apparently been determined by structure joints in the granite. The gable on the northeast end is magnificent in size and simplicity, and at its base there is a big snow-bank protected by the shadow of the building. The front is adorned with many pinnacles and a tall spire of curious workmanship. Here too the joints in the rock are seen to have played an important part in determining their forms and size and general arrangement. The Cathedral is said to be about 11,000 feet above the sea, but the height of the building itself above the level of the ridge it stands on is about 1500 feet. A mile or so to the westward there is a handsome lake, and the glacier-polished granite about it is shining so brightly it is not easy in some places to trace the line between the rock and water, both shining alike. Of this lake with its silvery basin and bits of meadow and groves I have a fine view from the spires; also of Lake Tenaya, Cloud's Rest and the South Dome of Yosemite, Mount Starr King, Mount Hoffman, the Merced peaks, and the vast multitude of snowy fountain peaks extending far north and south along the axis of the range. No feature, however, of all the noble landscape as seen from here seems more wonderful than the Cathedral itself, a temple displaying Nature's best masonry and sermons in stones. How often I have gazed at it from the tops of hills and ridges, and through openings in the forests on my many short excursions, devoutly wondering, admiring, longing! This I may say is the first time I have been at church in California, led here at last, every door graciously opened for the poor lonely worshipper. In our best times everything turns into religion, all the world seems a church and the mountains altars. And lo, here at last in front of the Cathedral is blessed cassiope, ringing her thousands of sweet-toned bells, the sweetest church music I ever enjoyed. Listening, admiring, until late in the afternoon I compelled myself to hasten away eastward back of rough, sharp, spiry, splintery peaks, all of them granite like the Cathedral, sparkling with crystals – feldspar, quartz, hornblende, mica, tourmaline. Had a rather difficult walk and creep across an immense snow and ice cliff which gradually increased in steepness as I advanced until it was almost impassable. Slipped on a dangerous place, but managed to stop by digging my heels into the thawing surface just on the brink of a yawning ice gulf. Camped beside a little pool and a group of crinkled dwarf pines; and as I sit by the fire trying to write notes the shallow pool seems fathomless with the infinite starry heavens in it, while the onlooking rocks and trees, tiny shrubs and daisies and sedges, brought forward in the fire-glow, seem full of thought as if about to speak aloud and tell all their wild stories. A marvellously impressive meeting in which every one has something worthwhile to tell. And beyond the fire-beams out in the solemn darkness, how impressive is the music of a choir of rills singing their way down from the snow to the river! And when we call to mind that thousands of these rejoicing rills are assembled in each one of the main streams, we wonder the less that our Sierra rivers are songful all the way to the sea.

About sundown saw a flock of dun greyish sparrows going to roost in crevices of a crag above the big snow-field. Charming little mountaineers! Found a species of sedge in flower within eight or ten feet of a snow-bank. Judging by the looks of the ground, it can hardly have been out in the sunshine much longer than a week, and it is likely to be buried again in fresh snow in a month or so, thus making a winter about ten months long, while spring, summer, and autumn are crowded and hurried into two months. How delightful it is to be alone here! How wild everything is – wild as the sky and as pure! Never shall I forget this big, divine day – the Cathedral and its thousands of cassiope bells, and the landscapes around them, and this camp in the grey crags above the woods, with its stars and streams and snow.

September 8. Day of climbing, scrambling, sliding on the peaks around the highest source of the Tuolumne and Merced. Climbed three of the most commanding of the mountains, whose names I don't know; crossed streams and huge beds of ice and snow more than I could keep count of. Neither could I keep count of the lakes scattered on tablelands and in the cirques of the peaks, and in chains in the canyons, linked together by the streams – a tremendously wild grey wilderness of hacked, shattered crags, ridges, and peaks, a few clouds drifting over and through the midst of them as if looking for work. In general views all the immense round landscape seems raw and lifeless as a quarry, yet the most charming flowers were found rejoicing in countless nooks and garden-like patches everywhere. I must have done three or four days' climbing work in this one. Limbs perfectly tireless until near sun-down, when I descended into the main upper Tuolumne valley at the foot of Mount Lyell, the camp still eight or ten miles distant. Going up through the pine woods past the Soda Springs Dome in the dark, where there is much fallen timber, and when all the excitement of seeing things was wanting, I was tired. Arrived at the main camp at nine o'clock, and soon was sleeping sound as death.

5

A NEAR VIEW
OF THE HIGH SIERRA

John Muir

This abstract describes Muir's epic first ascent of Mount Ritter in 1872, during a journey on which he led three artists on a sketching trip to the mountains. It was later published in Muir's first book, *The Mountains of California*.

Early one bright morning in the middle of Indian summer, while the glacier meadows were still crisp with frost crystals, I set out from the foot of Mount Lyell, on my way down to Yosemite Valley, to replenish my exhausted store of bread and tea. I had spent the past summer, as many preceding ones, exploring the glaciers that lie on the head waters of the San Joaquin, Tuolumne, Merced, and Owen's Rivers; measuring and studying their movements, trends, crevasses, moraines, etc., and the part they had played during the period of their greater extension in the creation and development of the landscapes of this alpine wonderland. The time for this kind of work was nearly over for the year, and I began to look forward with delight to the approaching winter with its wondrous storms, when I would be warmly snowbound in my Yosemite cabin with plenty of bread and books; but a tinge of regret came on when I considered that possibly I might not see this favourite region again until the next summer, excepting distant views from the heights about the Yosemite walls.

To artists, few portions of the High Sierra are, strictly speaking, picturesque. The whole massive uplift of the range is one great picture, not clearly divisible into smaller ones; differing much in this respect from the older, and what may be called, riper mountains of the Coast Range. All the landscapes of the Sierra, as we have seen, were born again, remodelled from base to summit by the developing ice floods of the last glacial winter. But all these new landscapes were not brought forth simultaneously; some of the highest, where the ice lingered longest, are tens of centuries younger than those of the warmer regions below them. In general, the younger the mountain landscapes, – younger, I mean, with reference to the time of their emergence from the ice of the glacial period, – the less separable are they into artistic bits capable of being made into warm, sympathetic, loveable pictures with appreciable humanity in them.

Here, however, on the head waters of the Tuolumne, is a group of wild peaks on which the geologist may say that the sun has but just begun to shine, which is yet in a high degree picturesque, and in its main features so regular and evenly balanced as almost to appear conventional – one sombre cluster of snow-laden peaks with grey, pine-fringed, granite bosses braided around its base, the whole surging free into the sky from the head of a magnificent valley, whose lofty walls are bevelled away on both sides so as to embrace it all without admitting anything not strictly belonging to it. The foreground was now aflame with autumn colours, brown and purple and gold, ripe in the mellow sunshine; contrasting brightly with the deep, cobalt blue of the sky, and the black and grey, and pure, spiritual white of the rocks and glaciers. Down through the midst, the young Tuolumne was seen pouring from its crystal fountains, now resting in glassy pools as if changing back again into ice, now leaping in white cascades as if turning to snow; gliding right and left between granite bosses, then sweeping on through the smooth, meadowy levels of the valley, swaying pensively from side to side with calm, stately gestures past dipping willows and sedges, and around groves of arrowy pine; and throughout its whole eventful course, whether flowing fast or slow, singing loud or low, ever filling the landscape with spiritual animation, and manifesting the grandeur of its sources in every movement and tone.

Pursuing my lonely way down the valley, I turned again and again to gaze on the glorious picture, throwing up my arms to enclose it as in a frame. After long ages of growth in the darkness beneath the glaciers, through sunshine and storms, it seemed now to be ready and waiting for the elected artist, like yellow wheat for the reaper; and I could not help wishing that I might carry colours and brushes with me on my travels, and learn to paint. In the meantime I had to be content with photographs on my mind and sketches in my notebooks. At length, after I had rounded a precipitous headland that puts out from the west wall of the valley, every peak vanished from sight, and I pushed rapidly along the frozen meadows, over the divide between the waters of the Merced and Tuolumne, and down through the forests that clothe the slopes of Cloud's Rest, arriving in Yosemite in due time – which, with me, is *any* time. And, strange to say, among the first people I met here were two artists who, with letters of introduction, were awaiting my return. They enquired whether in the course of my explorations in the adjacent mountains I had ever come upon a landscape suitable for a large painting; whereupon I began a description of the one that had so lately excited my admiration. Then, as I went on further and further into details, their faces began to glow, and I offered to guide them to it, while they declared that they would gladly follow, far or near, whithersoever I could spare the time to lead them.

Since storms might come breaking down through the fine weather at any time, burying the colours in snow, and cutting off the artists' retreat, I advised getting ready at once.

I led them out of the valley by the Vernal and Nevada Falls, thence over the main dividing ridge to the Big Tuolumne Meadows, by the old Mono Trail, and thence along the Upper Tuolumne River to its head. This was my companions' first excursion into the High Sierra, and as I was almost always alone in my mountaineering, the way that the fresh beauty was reflected in their faces made for me a novel and interesting study. They naturally were affected most of all by the colours – the intense azure of the sky, the purplish greys of the granite, the red and browns of dry meadows, and the translucent purple and crimson of huckleberry bogs; the flaming yellow of aspen groves, the silvery flashing of the streams, and the bright green and blue of the glacier lakes. But the general expression of the scenery – rocky and savage – seemed sadly disappointing; and as they threaded the forest from ridge to ridge, eagerly scanning the landscapes as they were unfolded, they said: 'All this is huge and sublime, but we see nothing as yet at all available for effective pictures. Art is long, and art is limited, you know; and here are foregrounds, middle-grounds, backgrounds, all alike; bare rock waves, woods, groves, diminutive flecks of meadow, and strips of glittering water.'

'Never mind,' I replied, 'only bide a wee, and I will show you something you will like.'

At length, toward the end of the second day, the Sierra Crown began to come into view, and when we had fairly rounded the projecting headland before mentioned, the whole picture stood revealed in the flush of the alpenglow. Their enthusiasm was excited beyond bounds, and the more impulsive of the two, a young Scotchman,[1] dashed ahead, shouting and gesticulating and tossing his arms in the air like a madman. Here, at last, was a typical alpine landscape.

After feasting a while on the view, I proceeded to make camp in a sheltered grove a little way back from the meadow, where pine boughs could be obtained for beds, and where there was plenty of dry wood for fires, while the artists ran here and there, along the river bends and up the sides of the canyon, choosing foregrounds for sketches. After dark, when our tea was made and a rousing fire had been built, we began to make our plans. They decided to remain several days, at the least, while I concluded to make an excursion in the meantime to the untouched summit of Ritter.

It was now about the middle of October, the springtime of snow-flowers. The first winter clouds had already bloomed, and the peaks were strewn with fresh crystals without, however, affecting the climbing to any dangerous extent. And as the weather was still profoundly calm, and the distance to the foot of the mountain only a little more than a day, I felt that I was running no great risk of being storm-bound.

Mount Ritter is king of the mountains of the middle portion of the High Sierra, as Shasta of the north and Whitney of the south sections. Moreover, as far as I know, it had never been climbed. I had explored the adjacent wilderness summer after summer, but my studies thus far had never drawn me to the top of it. Its height above sea-level is about 13,300 feet, and it is fenced round by steeply inclined glaciers, and canyons of tremendous depth and ruggedness, which render it almost inaccessible. But difficulties of this kind only exhilarate the mountaineer.

A Near View of the High Sierra

Next morning, the artists went heartily to their work and I to mine. Former experiences had given good reason to know that passionate storms, invisible as yet, might be brooding in the calm sungold; therefore, before bidding farewell, I warned the artists not to be alarmed should I fail to appear before a week or ten days, and advised them, in case a snowstorm should set in, to keep up big fires and shelter themselves as best they could, and on no account to become frightened and attempt to seek their way back to Yosemite alone through the drifts.

My general plan was simply this: to scale the canyon wall, cross over to the eastern flank of the range, and then make my way southward to the northern spurs of Mount Ritter in compliance with the intervening topography; for to push on directly southward from camp through the innumerable peaks and pinnacles that adorn this portion of the axis of the range, however interesting, would take too much time, besides being extremely difficult and dangerous at this time of year.

All my first day was pure pleasure; simply mountaineering indulgence, crossing the dry pathways of the ancient glaciers, tracing happy streams, and learning the habits of the birds and marmots in the groves and rocks. Before I had gone a mile from camp, I came to the foot of a white cascade that beats its way down a rugged gorge in the canyon wall, from a height of about 900 feet, and pours its throbbing waters into the Tuolumne. I was acquainted with its fountains, which, fortunately, lay in my course. What a fine travelling companion it proved to be, what songs it sang, and how passionately it told the mountain's own joy! Gladly I climbed along its dashing border, absorbing its divine music, and bathing from time to time in waftings of irised spray. Climbing higher, higher, new beauty came streaming on the sight: painted meadows, late-blooming gardens, peaks of rare architecture, lakes here and there, shining like silver, and glimpses of the forested middle region and the yellow lowlands far in the west. Beyond the range I saw the so-called Mono Desert, lying dreamily silent in thick purple light – a desert of heavy sun-glare beheld from a desert of ice-burnished granite. Here the waters divide, shouting in glorious enthusiasm, and falling eastward to vanish in the volcanic sands and dry sky of the Great Basin, or westward to the

Great Valley of California, and thence through the Bay of San Francisco and the Golden Gate to the sea.

Passing a little way down over the summit until I had reached an elevation of about 10,000 feet, I pushed on southward toward a group of savage peaks that stand guard about Ritter on the north and west, groping my way, and dealing instinctively with every obstacle as it presented itself. Here a huge gorge would be found cutting across my path, along the dizzy edge of which I scrambled until some less precipitous point was discovered where I might safely venture to the bottom and then, selecting some feasible portion of the opposite wall, re-ascend with the same slow caution. Massive, flat-topped spurs alternate with the gorges, plunging abruptly from the shoulders of the snowy peaks, and planting their feet in the warm desert. These were everywhere marked and adorned with characteristic sculptures of the ancient glaciers that swept over this entire region like one vast ice wind, and the polished surfaces produced by the ponderous flood are still so perfectly preserved that in many places the sunlight reflected from them is about as trying to the eyes as sheets of snow.

God's glacial mills grind slowly, but they have been kept in motion long enough in California to grind sufficient soil for a glorious abundance of life, though most of the grist has been carried to the lowlands, leaving these high regions comparatively lean and bare; while the post-glacial agents of erosion have not yet furnished sufficient available food over the general surface for more than a few tufts of the hardiest plants, chiefly carices and eriogonæ. And it is interesting to learn in this connection that the sparseness and repressed character of the vegetation at this height is caused more by want of soil than by harshness of climate; for, here and there, in sheltered hollows (countersunk beneath the general surface) into which a few rods of well-ground moraine chips have been dumped, we find groves of spruce and pine thirty to forty feet high, trimmed around the edges with willow and huckleberry bushes, and often-times still further by an outer ring of tall grasses, bright with lupines, larkspurs, and showy columbines, suggesting a climate by no means repressingly severe. All the streams, too, and the pools at this elevation are furnished with little gardens wherever soil can be made to lie, which, though making scarce any show at a distance, constitute charming surprises to the appreciative observer. In these bits of leafiness a few birds find grateful homes. Having no acquaintance with man, they fear no ill, and flock curiously about the stranger, almost allowing themselves to be taken in the hand. In so wild and so beautiful a region was spent my first day, every sight and sound inspiring, leading one far out of himself, yet feeding and building up his individuality.

Now came the solemn, silent evening. Long, blue, spiky shadows crept out across the snow-fields, while a rosy glow, at first scarce discernible, gradually deepened and suffused every mountain-top, flushing the glaciers and the harsh crags above them. This was the alpenglow, to me one of the most impressive of all the terrestrial manifestations of God. At the touch of this divine light, the mountains seemed to kindle to a rapt, religious consciousness, and stood hushed and waiting like devout worshippers. Just before the alpenglow began to fade, two crimson clouds came streaming across the summit like wings of flame, rendering the sublime scene yet more impressive; then came darkness and the stars.

Icy Ritter was still miles away, but I could proceed no farther that night. I found a good camp-ground on the rim of a glacier basin about 11,000 feet above the sea. A small lake nestles in the bottom of it, from which I got water for my tea, and a storm-beaten thicket nearby furnished abundance of resiny firewood. Sombre peaks, hacked and shattered, circled halfway around the horizon, wearing a savage aspect in the gloaming, and a waterfall chanted solemnly across the lake on its way down from the foot of a glacier. The fall and the lake and the glacier were almost equally bare; while the scraggy pines anchored in the rock-fissures were so dwarfed and shorn by storm-winds that you might walk over their tops. In tone and aspect the scene was one of the most desolate I ever beheld. But the darkest scriptures of the mountains are illumined with bright passages of love that never fail to make themselves felt when one is alone.

I made my bed in a nook of the pine thicket, where the branches were pressed and crinkled overhead like a roof, and bent down around the sides. These are the best bedchambers the high mountains afford – snug as squirrel nests, well-ventilated, full of spicy odours, and with plenty of wind-played needles to sing one asleep. I little expected company, but, creeping in through a low side door, I found five or six birds nestling among the tassels. The night wind began to blow soon after dark; at first only a gentle breathing, but increasing toward midnight to a rough gale that fell upon my leafy roof in ragged surges like a cascade, bearing wild sounds from the crags overhead. The waterfall sang in chorus, filling the old ice fountain with its solemn roar, and seeming to increase in power as the night advanced – fit voice for such a landscape. I had to creep out many times to the fire during the night, for it was biting cold and I had no blankets. Gladly I welcomed the morning star.

The dawn in the dry, wavering air of the desert was glorious. Everything encouraged my undertaking and betokened success. There was no cloud in the sky, no storm tone in the wind. Breakfast of bread and tea was soon made. I fastened a hard, durable crust to my belt by way of provision, in case I should be compelled to pass a night on the mountain-top; then, securing the remainder of my little stock against wolves and wood rats, I set forth free and hopeful.

How glorious a greeting the sun gives the mountains! To behold this alone is worth the pains of any excursion a thousand times over. The highest peaks burned like islands in a sea of liquid shade. Then the lower peaks and spires caught the glow, and long lances of light, streaming through many a notch and pass, fell thick on the frozen meadows. The majestic form of Ritter was full in sight, and I pushed rapidly on over rounded rock bosses and pavements, my iron-shod shoes making a clanking sound, suddenly hushed now and then in rugs of bryanthus, and sedgy lake margins soft as moss. Here, too, in this so-called 'land of desolation', I met cassiope, growing in fringes among the battered rocks. Her blossoms had faded long ago, but they were still clinging with happy memories to the evergreen sprays, and still so beautiful as to thrill every fibre of one's being. Winter and summer, you may hear her voice, the low, sweet melody of her purple bells. No evangel among all the mountain plants speaks Nature's love more plainly than cassiope. Where she dwells, the redemption of the coldest solitude is complete. The very rocks and glaciers seem to feel her presence, and become imbued with her own fountain sweetness. All things were warming and awakening. Frozen rills began to flow, the marmots came out of their nests in boulder piles and climbed sunny rocks to bask, and the dun-headed sparrows were flitting about seeking their breakfasts. The lakes seen from every ridge-top were brilliantly rippled and spangled, shimmering like the thickets of the low dwarf pines. The rocks, too, seemed responsive to the vital heat – rock crystals and snow crystals thrilling alike. I strode on exhilarated, as if never more to feel fatigue, limbs moving of themselves, every sense unfolding like the thawing flowers, to take part in the new day harmony.

All along my course thus far, excepting when down in the canyons, the landscapes were mostly open to me, and expansive, at least on one side. On the left were the purple plains of Mono, reposing dreamily and warm; on the right, the near peaks springing keenly into the thin sky with more and more impressive sublimity. But these larger views were at length lost. Rugged spurs, and moraines, and huge, projecting buttresses began to shut me in. Every feature became more rigidly alpine, without, however, producing any chilling effect; for going to the mountains is like going home. We always find that the strangest objects in these fountain wilds are in some degree familiar, and we look upon them with a vague sense of having seen them before.

On the southern shore of a frozen lake, I encountered an extensive field of hard, granular snow, up which I scampered in fine tone, intending to follow it to its head, and cross the rocky spur against which it leans, hoping thus to come direct upon the base of the main Ritter peak. The surface was pitted with oval hollows, made by stones and drifted pine needles that had melted themselves into the mass by the radiation of absorbed sun-heat. These afforded good footholds, but the surface curved more and more steeply at the head, and the pits became shallower and less abundant, until I found myself in danger of being shed off like avalanching snow. I persisted, however, creeping on all fours, and shuffling up the smoothest places on my back, as I had often done on burnished granite, until, after slipping several times, I was compelled to retrace my course to the bottom, and made my way around the west end of the lake, and thence up to the summit of the divide between the head waters of Rush Creek and the northernmost tributaries of the San Joaquin.

Arriving on the summit of this dividing crest, one of the most exciting pieces of pure wilderness was disclosed that I ever discovered in all my mountaineering. There, immediately in front, loomed the majestic mass of Mount Ritter, with a glacier swooping down its face nearly to my feet, then curving westward and pouring its frozen flood into a dark blue lake, whose shores were bound with precipices of crystalline snow; while a deep chasm drawn between the divide and the glacier separated the massive picture from everything else. I could see only the one sublime mountain, the one glacier, the one lake; the whole veiled with one blue shadow – rock, ice, and water close together, without a single leaf or sign of life. After gazing spellbound, I began instinctively to scrutinise every notch and gorge and weathered buttress of the mountain, with reference to making the ascent. The entire front above the glacier appeared as one tremendous precipice, slightly receding at the top, and bristling with spires and pinnacles set above one another in formidable array. Massive lichen-stained battlements stood forward here and there, hacked at the top with angular notches, and separated by frosty gullies and recesses that have been veiled in shadow ever since their creation; while to right and left, as far as I could see, were huge, crumbling buttresses, offering no hope to the climber. The head of the glacier sends up a few finger-like branches through narrow couloirs; but these seemed too steep and short to be available, especially as I had no axe with which to cut steps, and the numerous narrow-throated gullies down which stones and snow are avalanched seemed hopelessly steep, besides being interrupted by vertical cliffs; while the whole front was rendered still more terribly forbidding by the chill shadow and the gloomy blackness of the rocks.

Descending the divide in a hesitating mood, I picked my way across the yawning chasm at the foot, and climbed out upon the glacier. There were no meadows now to cheer with their brave colours, nor could I hear the dun-headed sparrows, whose cheery notes so often relieve the silence of our highest mountains. The only sounds were the gurgling of small rills down in the veins and crevasses of the glacier, and now and then the rattling report of falling stones, with the echoes they shot out into the crisp air.

I could not distinctly hope to reach the summit from this side, yet I moved on across the glacier as if driven by fate. Contending with myself, the season is too far spent, I said, and even should I be successful, I might be storm-bound on the mountain; and in the cloud darkness, with the cliffs and crevasses covered with snow, how could I escape? No; I must wait till next summer. I would only approach the mountain now, and inspect it, creep about its flanks, learn what I could of its history, holding myself ready to flee on the approach of the first storm cloud. But we little know until tried how much of the uncontrollable there is in us, urging over glaciers and torrents, and up perilous heights, let the judgement forbid as it may.

I succeeded in gaining the foot of the cliff on the eastern extremity of the glacier, and there discovered the mouth of a narrow avalanche gully, through which I began to climb, intending to follow it as far as possible, and at least obtain some fine wild views for my pains. Its general course is oblique to the plane of the mountain-face, and the metamorphic slates of which the mountain is built are cut by cleavage planes in such a way that they weather off in angular blocks, giving rise to irregular steps that greatly facilitate climbing on the sheer places. I thus made my way into a wilderness of crumbling spires and battlements, built together in bewildering combinations, and glazed in many places with a thin coating of ice, which I had to hammer off with stones. The situation was becoming gradually more perilous; but, having passed several dangerous spots, I dared not think of descending; for, so steep was the entire ascent, one would inevitably fall to the glacier in case a single misstep were made. Knowing, therefore, the tried danger beneath, I became all the more anxious concerning the developments to be made above, and began to be conscious of a vague foreboding of what actually befell; not that I was given to fear, but rather because my instincts, usually so positive and true, seemed vitiated in some way, and were leading me astray. At length, after attaining an elevation of about 12,800 feet, I found myself at the foot of a sheer drop in the bed of the avalanche channel I was tracing, which seemed absolutely to bar further progress. It was only about forty-five or fifty feet high, and somewhat roughened by fissures and projections; but these seemed so slight and insecure, as footholds, that I tried hard to avoid the precipice altogether, by scaling the wall of the channel on either side. But, though less steep, the walls were smoother than the obstructing rock, and repeated efforts only showed that I must either go right ahead or turn back.

The tried dangers beneath seemed even greater than that of the cliff in front; therefore, after scanning its face again and again, I began to scale it, picking my holds with intense caution. After gaining a point about halfway to the top, I was suddenly brought to a dead stop, with arms outspread, clinging close to the face of the rock, unable to move hand or foot either up or down. My doom appeared fixed. I *must* fall. There would be a moment of bewilderment, and then a lifeless rumble down the one general precipice to the glacier below.

When this final danger flashed upon me, I became nerve-shaken for the first time since setting foot on the mountains, and my mind seemed to fill with a stifling smoke. But this terrible eclipse lasted only a moment, when life blazed forth again with preternatural clearness. I seemed suddenly to become possessed of a new sense. The other self, bygone experiences, Instinct, or Guardian Angel, – call it what you will, – came forward and assumed control. Then my trembling muscles became firm again, every rift and flaw in the rock was seen as through a microscope, and my limbs moved with a positiveness and precision with which I seemed to have nothing at all to do. Had I been borne aloft upon wings, my deliverance could not have been more complete.

Above this memorable spot, the face of the mountain is still more savagely hacked and torn. It is a maze of yawning chasms and gullies, in the angles of which rise beetling crags and piles of detached boulders that seem to have been gotten ready to be launched below. But the strange influx of strength I had received seemed inexhaustible. I found a way without effort, and soon stood upon the topmost crag in the blessed light.

How truly glorious the landscape circled around this noble summit! – giant mountains, valleys innumerable, glaciers and meadows, rivers and lakes, with the wide blue sky bent tenderly over them all. But in my first hour of freedom from that terrible shadow, the sunlight in which I was laving seemed all in all.

Looking southward along the axis of the range, the eye is first caught by a row of exceedingly sharp and slender spires, which rise openly to a height of about a 1000 feet, above a series of short, residual glaciers that lean back against their bases; their fantastic sculpture and the unrelieved sharpness with which they spring out of the ice rendering them peculiarly wild and striking. These are 'The Minarets'. Beyond them you behold a sublime wilderness of mountains, their snowy summits towering together in crowded abundance, peak beyond peak, swelling higher, higher, as they sweep on southward, until the culminating point of the range is reached on Mount Whitney, near the head of the Kern River, at an elevation of nearly 14,700 feet above the level of the sea.

Westward, the general flank of the range is seen flowing sublimely away from the sharp summits, in smooth undulations; a sea of huge grey granite waves dotted with lakes and meadows, and fluted with stupendous canyons that grow steadily deeper as they recede in the distance. Below this grey region lies the dark forest zone, broken here and there by upswelling ridges and domes; and yet beyond lies a yellow, hazy belt, marking the broad plain of the San Joaquin, bounded on its farther side by the blue mountains of the coast.

Turning now to the northward, there in the immediate foreground is the glorious Sierra Crown, with Cathedral Peak, a temple of marvellous architecture, a few degrees to the left of it; the grey, massive form of Mammoth Mountain to the right; while Mounts Ord, Gibbs, Dana, Conness, Tower Peak, Castle Peak, Silver Mountain, and a host of noble companions, as yet nameless, make a sublime show along the axis of the range.

Eastward, the whole region seems a land of desolation covered with beautiful light. The torrid volcanic basin of Mono, with its one bare lake fourteen miles long; Owen's Valley and the broad lava tableland at its head, dotted with craters, and the massive Inyo Range, rivalling even the Sierra in height; these are spread, map-like, beneath you, with countless ranges beyond, passing and overlapping one another and fading on the glowing horizon.

At a distance of less than 3000 feet below the summit of Mount Ritter you may find tributaries of the San Joaquin and Owen's Rivers, bursting forth from the ice and snow of the glaciers that load its flanks; while a little to the north of here are found the highest affluents of the Tuolumne and Merced. Thus, the fountains of four of the principal rivers of California are within a radius of four or five miles.

Lakes are seen gleaming in all sorts of places, – round, or oval, or square, like very mirrors; others narrow and sinuous, drawn close around the peaks like silver zones, the highest reflecting only rocks, snow, and the sky. But neither these nor the glaciers, nor the bits of brown meadow and moorland that occur here and there, are large enough to make any marked impression upon the mighty wilderness of mountains. The eye, rejoicing in its freedom, roves about the vast expanse, yet returns again and again to the fountain peaks. Perhaps some one of the multitude excites special attention, some gigantic castle with turret and battlement, or some Gothic cathedral more abundantly spired than Milan's. But, generally, when looking for the first time from an all-embracing standpoint like this, the inexperienced observer is oppressed by the incomprehensible grandeur, variety, and abundance of the mountains rising shoulder to shoulder beyond the reach of vision; and it is only after they have been studied one by one, long and lovingly, that their far-reaching harmonies become manifest. Then, penetrate the wilderness where you may, the main telling features, to which all the surrounding topography is subordinate, are quickly perceived, and the most complicated clusters of peaks stand revealed harmoniously correlated and fashioned like works of art – eloquent monuments of the ancient ice rivers that brought them into relief from the general mass of the range. The canyons, too, some of them a mile deep, mazing wildly through the mighty host of mountains, however lawless and ungovernable at first sight they appear, are at length recognised as the necessary effects of causes which followed each other in harmonious sequence – Nature's poems carved on tables of stone – simplest and most emphatic of her glacial compositions.

Could we have been here to observe during the glacial period, we should have overlooked a wrinkled ocean of ice as continuous as that now covering the landscapes of Greenland; filling every valley and canyon with only the tops of the fountain peaks rising darkly above the rock-encumbered ice waves like islets in a stormy sea – those islets the only hints of the glorious landscapes now smiling in the sun. Standing here in the deep, brooding silence all the wilderness seems motionless, as if the work of creation were done. But in the midst of this outer steadfastness we know there is incessant motion and change. Ever and anon, avalanches are falling from yonder peaks.

These cliff-bound glaciers, seemingly wedged and immovable, are flowing like water and grinding the rocks beneath them. The lakes are lapping their granite shores and wearing them away, and every one of these rills and young rivers is fretting the air into music, and carrying the mountains to the plains. Here are the roots of all the life of the valleys, and here more simply than elsewhere is the eternal flux of Nature manifested. Ice changing to water, lakes to meadows, and mountains to plains. And while we thus contemplate Nature's methods of landscape creation, and, reading the records she has carved on the rocks, reconstruct, however imperfectly, the landscapes of the past, we also learn that as these we now behold have succeeded those of the pre-glacial age, so they in turn are withering and vanishing to be succeeded by others yet unborn.

But in the midst of these fine lessons and landscapes, I had to remember that the sun was wheeling far to the west, while a new way down the mountain had to be discovered to some point on the timber line where I could have a fire; for I had not even burdened myself with a coat. I first scanned the western spurs, hoping some way might appear through which I might reach the northern glacier, and cross its snout, or pass around the lake into which it flows, and thus strike my morning track. This route was soon sufficiently unfolded to show that, if it were practicable at all, it would require so much time that reaching camp that night would be out of the question. I therefore scrambled back eastward, and descended the southern slopes obliquely at the same time. Here the crags seemed less formidable, and the head of a glacier that flows northeast came in sight, which I determined to follow as far as possible, hoping thus to make my way to the foot of the peak on the east side, and thence across the intervening canyons and ridges to camp.

The inclination of the glacier is quite moderate at the head, and, as the sun had softened the névé, I made safe and rapid progress, running and sliding, and keeping up a sharp outlook for crevasses. About half a mile from the head, there is an ice cascade, where the glacier pours over a sharp declivity and is shattered into massive blocks separated by deep, blue fissures. To thread my way through the slippery mazes of this crevassed portion seemed impossible, and I endeavoured to avoid it by climbing off to the shoulder of the mountain. But the slopes rapidly steepened and at length fell away in sheer precipices, compelling a return to the ice. Fortunately, the day had been warm enough to loosen the ice crystals so as to admit of hollows being dug in the rotten portions of the blocks, thus enabling me to pick my way with far less difficulty than I had anticipated. Continuing down over the snout, and along the left lateral moraine, was only a confident saunter, showing that the ascent of the mountain by way of this glacier is easy, provided one is armed with an axe to cut steps here and there.

The lower end of the glacier was beautifully waved and barred by the outcropping edges of the bedded ice layers which represent the annual snowfalls, and to some extent the irregularities of structure caused by the weathering of the walls of crevasses, and by separate snowfalls which have been followed by rain, hail, thawing and freezing, etc. Small rills were gliding and swirling over the melting surface with a smooth, oily appearance, in channels of pure ice – their quick, compliant movements contrasting most impressively with the rigid, invisible flow of the glacier itself, on whose back they all were riding.

Night drew near before I reached the eastern base of the mountain, and my camp lay many a rugged mile to the north; but ultimate success was assured. It was now only a matter of endurance and ordinary mountaincraft. The sunset was, if possible, yet more beautiful than that of the day before. The Mono landscape seemed to be fairly saturated with warm, purple light. The peaks marshalled along the summit were in shadow, but through every notch and pass streamed vivid sunfire, soothing and irradiating their rough, black angles, while companies of small, luminous clouds hovered above them like very angels of light.

Darkness came on, but I found my way by the trends of the canyons and the peaks projected against the sky. All excitement died with the light, and then I was weary. But the joyful sound of the waterfall across the lake was heard at last, and soon the stars were seen reflected in the lake itself. Taking my bearings from these, I discovered the little pine thicket in which my nest was, and then I had a rest such as only a tired mountaineer may enjoy. After lying loose and lost for a while, I made a sunrise fire, went down to the lake, dashed water on my head, and dipped a cupful for tea. The revival brought about by bread and tea was as complete as the exhaustion from excessive enjoyment and toil. Then I crept beneath the pine tassels to bed. The wind was frosty and the fire burned low, but my sleep was none the less sound, and the evening constellations had swept far to the west before I awoke.

After thawing and resting in the morning sunshine, I sauntered home, – that is, back to the Tuolumne camp, – bearing away toward a cluster of peaks that hold the fountain snows of one of the north tributaries of Rush Creek. Here I discovered a group of beautiful glacier lakes, nestled together in a grand amphitheatre. Toward evening, I crossed the divide separating the Mono waters from those of the Tuolumne, and entered the glacier basin that now holds the fountain snows of the stream that forms the upper Tuolumne cascades. This stream I traced down through its many dells and gorges, meadows and bogs, reaching the brink of the main Tuolumne at dusk.

A loud whoop for the artists was answered again and again. Their campfire came in sight, and half an hour afterward I was with them. They seemed unreasonably glad to see me. I had been absent only three days; nevertheless, though the weather was fine, they had already been weighing chances as to whether I would ever return, and trying to decide whether they should wait longer or begin to seek their way back to the lowlands. Now their curious troubles were over. They packed their precious sketches, and next morning we set out homeward bound, and in two days entered the Yosemite Valley from the north by way of Indian Canyon.

NOTES:
1. This was Muir's first meeting with the artist William Keith, a native of Old Meldrum in Aberdeenshire, Scotland. Keith was born in 1838, the same year as Muir, and emigrated to the United States in the same year of 1849; he went on to become the best-known California landscape painter and was awarded the title 'Old Master of California'.

   Keith became a life-long friend and accompanied Muir to the summit of Mt Rainier in their ascent of 1888, when both were fifty years of age.

6

MOUNTAIN THOUGHTS

John Muir

These fragments, thought to have been written during Muir's first
years in Yosemite, were gathered together by Linnie Marsh Wolfe and
published in *John of the Mountains* in 1938.

The Sierra

Mountains holy as Sinai. No mountains I know of are so alluring.
None so hospitable, kindly, tenderly inspiring. It seems strange that
everybody does not come at their call. They are given, like the
Gospel, without money and without price. 'Tis heaven alone that is
given away.

Here is calm so deep, grasses cease waving.

Wonderful how completely everything in wild nature fits into us,
as if truly part and parent of us. The sun shines not on us but in us.
The rivers flow not past, but through us, thrilling, tingling, vibrating
every fibre and cell of the substance of our bodies, making them glide
and sing. The trees wave and the flowers bloom in our bodies as well
as our souls, and every bird song, wind song, and tremendous storm
song of the rocks in the heart of the mountains is our song, our very
own, and sings our love.

The Song of God, sounding on forever. So pure and sure and
universal is the harmony, it matters not where we are, where we strike
in on the wild lowland plains. We care not to go to the mountains,
and on the mountains we care not to go to the plains. But as soon as
we are absorbed in the harmony, plain, mountain, calm, storm, lilies
and sequoias, forests and meads are only different strands of many-
coloured Light are one in the sunbeam!

What wonders lie in every mountain day!

Crystals of snow, plash of small raindrops, hum of small insects, booming beetles, the jolly rattle of grasshoppers, chirping crickets, the screaming of hawks, jays, and Clark crows, the coo-r-r-r of cranes, the honking of geese, partridges drumming, trumpeting swans, frogs croaking, the whirring rattle of snakes, the awful enthusiasm of booming falls, the roar of cataracts, the crash and roll of thunder, earthquake shocks, the whisper of rills soothing to slumber, the piping of marmots, the bark of squirrels, the laugh of a wolf, the snorting of deer, the explosive roaring of bears, the squeak of mice, the cry of the loon, loneliest, wildest of sounds.

A fine place for feasting if only one be poor enough. One is speedily absorbed into the spiritual values of things. The body vanishes and the freed soul goes abroad.

Only in the roar of storms do these mighty solitudes find voice at all commensurate with their grandeur . . . The pines at the approach of storms show eager expectancy, bowing, swishing, tossing their branches with eager gestures, roaring like lions about to be fed, standing bent and round-shouldered like sentinels exposed.

Sickness, pain death – yet who could guess their existence in this fresh, abounding, overflowing life, this universal beauty?

Race living on race, killers killed, yet how little we see of this slaughter! How neatly, secretly, decently is this killing done! I never saw one drop of blood, one red stain on all this wilderness. Even death is in harmony here. Only in shambles and the downy beds of homes is death terrible. Perhaps there is more pleasure than pain in natural death, or even violent death. Livingstone declared that the crushing of his arm by a lion was rather pleasurable than otherwise.

Bloody Canyon
Nature's darlings are cared for and caressed even here, and protected by a thousand miracles in the very home and brooding-places of storms.

Faint are the marks of any kind of life, and at first you cannot see them or feel them at all. But here is the blessed water-ouzel pleading, fluttering about amid the spray, and blending his sweet, small, human songs with those of the streams he loves so well. And many other birds who build their nests here, and the flowers with few leaves that bloom on the rocks as if fallen like snow from the sky.

And here the grasshopper jumps and springs his rattle, as if to say, who is afraid?

And the bumblebee singing every summer the songs sung a thousand years ago.

A flock of wild sheep move aloft on the crags of the walls, not lost and cast away, but seeming to say in fullness of strength and ease: 'Here we are fled, and here is our home and safe hiding-place.'

One thinks of the redmen with flesh coloured like the rocks, and sinews tough as the granite, who for thousands of years have dragged in files through these silent depths, clad in dull skins and grass, with mountain flowers stuck in their black hair and their wild animal eyes sparkling bright as the lakes.

Only the unimaginative can fail to feel the enchantment of these mountains.

Nothing is more wonderful than to find smooth harmony in this lofty cragged region where at first sight all seems so rough. From any of the high standpoints a thousand peaks, pinnacles, spires are seen thrust into the sky and so sheer and bare as to be inaccessible to wild sheep, accessible only to the eagle. Any one by itself harsh, rugged, crumbling, yet in connection with others seems like a line of writing along the sky; it melts into melody, one leading into another, keeping rhythm in time. The cleanness of the ground suggests Nature taking pains like a housewife, the rock pavements seem as if carefully swept and dusted and polished every day. No wonder one feels a magic exhilaration when these pavements are touched, when the manifold currents of life that flow through the pores of the rock are considered, that keep every crystal particle in rhythmic motion dancing. Tissiacks seldom have lofty domes to give grace to their strength. They are mostly stout, thickset mountains with spread bases for strength, because they have been born of two great streams and overflowed and much eroded. Glaciers eat their own offspring.

Books

I have a low opinion of books; they are but piles of stones set up to show coming travellers where other minds have been, or at best signal smokes to call attention. Cadmus and all the other inventors of letters receive a thousand-fold more credit than they deserve. No amount of word-making will ever make a single soul to *know* these mountains. As well seek to warm the naked and frost-bitten by lectures on caloric and pictures of flame. One day's exposure to mountains is better than cartloads of books. See how willingly Nature poses herself upon photographers' plates. No earthly chemicals are so sensitive as those of the human soul. All that is required is exposure, and purity of material. 'The pure in heart shall see God!'

Water Music

When in making our way through a forest we hear the loud boom of a waterfall, we know that the stream is descending a precipice. If a heavy rumble and roar, then we know it is passing over a craggy incline. But not only are the existence and size of these larger characters of its channel proclaimed, but all the others. Go to the fountain-canyons of the Merced. Some portions of its channel will appear smooth, others rough, here a slope, there a vertical wall, here a sandy meadow, there a lake-bowl, and the young river speaks and sings all the smaller characters of the smooth slope and downy hush of meadow as faithfully as it sings the great precipices and rapid inclines, so that anyone who has learned the language of running water will see its character in the dark.

Beside the grand history of the glaciers and their own, the mountain streams sing the history of every avalanche or earthquake and of snow, all easily recognised by the human ear, and every word evoked by the falling leaf and drinking deer, beside a thousand other facts so small and spoken by the stream in so low a voice the human ear cannot hear them. Thus every event is written and spoken. The wing scars the sky, making a path inevitably as the deer in snow, and the winds all know it and tell it though we hear it not.

We all know and wonder at the writing on the wall of the Persian king's palace, forgetting that there is a writing on every wall. Every glacier makes its mark, writes its history, and as we can read and recall the music of streams by going along their dry channels, so we can read the history of ice, the creature who above all others makes the heaviest mark, the largest track, and here the difficulty is not because of dimness, but because of magnitude, like an alphabet written too large. As tributary after tributary enters a trunk the channel is always increased to a corresponding degree. Winds and streams of water are the best interpreters and historians and preachers of ice now dead. Yosemite winds, Yosemite waters, glorious proclaimers, apostles of the combing ice, never cease to preach it night and day!

In snowstorms, flakes flicker and die in the lee of bare domes, or bear steadily aslant to their place on the white bosom of the sea.

Yosemite meadows in spring are covered with mirrors, small shallow lakelets that reflect with marvellous distinctness the over-looking mountains and every tree and bush and fine sculptured marking. These lakelets are memories of the great glacier lake of Yosemite, which, while the Tenaya Canyon above South Dome and the canyons of Illilouette and Nevada were yet blocked with ice, stretched its green waters from wall to wall. Its sublime rocks were reflected as now, but themselves, not yet dimmed with the rust of rains and snows, gleamed bright as the water. Gradually the lake was filled with the washed pebbles of its feeding streams, its waves were driven farther and yet farther from the walls, until at length only these mirrors are left to illustrate and enliven its history. Just as a man gradually fills to motionless rigidity by deposits from his life-supplying veins until like a sandy sediment-filled lake he rests in old age with only the main central river of life flowing through his body, yet with many a memory of the ardent days of youth.

We rode along the warm rim of Yosemite, to our left the mag-nificent battlements of the Hoffman and, on beyond, Cathedral Peak and its group of spires. Thick silence broods the Valley mansion. From the walls the splendid shafts of the pine, clustered and tall, rise stiffly as if to support the near low starry sky.

Some people miss flesh as a drunkard misses his dram. This depraved appetite stands greatly in the way of free days in the mountains, for meat of any kind is hard to carry, and makes a repulsive mess when jammed in a pack . . . So also the butter-and-milk habit has seized most people; bread without butter or coffee without milk is an awful calamity, as if everything before being put in our mouth must first be held under a cow. I know from long experience that all these things are unnecessary. One may take a little simple clean bread and have nothing to do on these fine excursions but enjoy oneself. *Vide* Thoreau. It seems ridiculous that a man, especially when in the midst of his best pleasures, should have to go beneath a cow like a calf three times a day – never weaned.

Indian Summer
Calm, thoughtful peace and hushed rest – the pause before passing into winter. The birds gathering to go, and the animals, warned by the night frosts, relining their nests with dry grass and leaves and thistledown.

The sun glowing red; the mountains silvery grey, purplish, one mass without detail, infinitely soft . . . The far-spreading meadows brown, yellow, and red. The river in the foreground silver between bosky willow-banks, green and orange and lemon yellow, every leaf and spray reflected in the mirror-water, its beauty doubled . . .

In the yellow mist the rough angles melt on the rocks. Forms, lines, tints, reflections, sounds, all are softened, and although the dying time, it is also the colour time, the time when faith in the steadfast-ness of Nature is surest . . . The seeds all have next summer in them, some of them thousands of summers, as the sequoia and cedar. In holiday array all go calmly down into the white winter rejoicing, plainly hopeful, faithful . . . everything taking what comes, and looking forward to the future, as if piously saying, 'Thy will be done in earth as in heaven!'

Spring
Quick-growing bloom days when sap flows fast like the swelling streams. Rising from the dead, the work of the year is pushed on with enthusiasm as if never done before, as if all God's glory depended upon it; inspiring every plant, bird, and stream to sing with youth's exuberance, painting flower petals, making leaf patterns, weaving a fresh roof – all symbols of eternal love.

Nature's literature is written in mountain-ranges along the sky, rising to heaven in triumphant songs in long ridge and dome and clustering peaks.

Mountains
When we dwell with mountains, see them face to face, every day, they seem as creatures with a sort of life – friends subject to moods, now talking, now taciturn, with whom we converse as man to man. They wear many spiritual robes, at times an aureole, something like the glory of the old painters put around the heads of saints. Especially is this seen on lone mountains, like Shasta, or on great domes standing single and apart.

Gain health from lusty, heroic exercise, from free, firm-nerved adventures without anxiety in them, with rhythmic leg motion in runs over boulders requiring quick decision for every step. Fording streams, tingling with flesh brushes as we slide down white slopes thatched with close snow-pressed chaparral, half swimming or flying or slipping – all these make good counter-irritants. Then enjoy the utter peace and solemnity of the trees and stars. Find many a plant and bird living sequestered in hollows and dells – little chambers in the hills. Feel a mysterious presence in a thousand coy hiding things.

Go free as the wind, living as true to Nature as those grey and buff people of the sequoias and the pines.

Wind
How far it has come, and how far it has to go! How many faces it has fanned, singing, skimming the levels of the sea; floating, sustaining the wide-winged gulls and albatrosses; searching the intricacies of the woods, taking up and carrying their fragrances to every living creature. Now stooping low, visiting the humblest flower, trying the temper of every leaf, tuning them, fondling and caressing them, stirring them in lusty exercise, carrying pollen from tree to tree, filling lakes with white lily spangles, chanting among pines, playing on every needle, on every mountain spire, on all the landscape as on a harp.

Go east, young man, go east! Californians have only to go east a few miles to be happy. Toilers on the heat plains, toilers in the cities by the sea, whose lives are well-nigh choked by the weeds of care that have grown up and run to seed about them – leave all and go east and you cannot escape a cure for all care. Earth hath no sorrows that earth cannot heal, or heaven cannot heal, for the earth as seen in the clean wilds of the mountains is about as divine as anything the heart of man can conceive!

7

PRAYERS IN THE HIGHER MOUNTAIN TEMPLES — OR A GEOLOGIST'S WINTER WALK

John Muir

This is an excerpt from a letter to Jeanne Carr, written in 1873, which was included in *Steep Trails*, edited by William Frederic Badè and published in 1918.

After reaching Turlock, I sped afoot over the stubble fields and through miles of brown hemizonia and purple erigeron, to Hopeton, conscious of little more than that the town was behind and beneath me, and the mountains above and before me; on through the oaks and chaparral of the foothills to Coulterville; and then ascended the first great mountain step upon which grows the sugar pine. Here I slackened pace, for I drank the spicy, resiny wind, and beneath the arms of this noble tree I felt that I was safely home. Never did pine trees seem so dear. How sweet was their breath and their song, and how grandly they winnowed the sky! I tingled my fingers among their tassels, and rustled my feet among their brown needles and burrs, and was exhilarated and joyful beyond all I can write.

When I reached Yosemite, all the rocks seemed talkative, and more telling and loveable than ever. They are dear friends, and seemed to have warm blood gushing through their granite flesh; and I love them with a love intensified by long and close companionship. After I had bathed in the bright river, sauntered over the meadows, conversed with the domes, and played with the pines, I still felt blurred and weary, as if tainted in some way with the sky of your streets. I determined, therefore, to run out for a while to say my prayers in the higher mountain temples. 'The days are sun-full,' I said, 'and, though now winter, no great danger need be encountered, and no sudden storm will block my return, if I am watchful.'

The morning after this decision, I started up the canyon of Tenaya, caring little about the quantity of bread I carried; for, I thought, a fast and a storm and a difficult canyon were just the medicine I needed. When I passed Mirror Lake, I scarcely noticed it, for I was absorbed in the great Tissiack – her crown a mile away in the hushed azure; her purple granite drapery flowing in soft and graceful folds down to my feet, embroidered gloriously around with deep, shadowy forest. I have gazed on Tissiack a thousand times – in days of solemn storms, and when her form shone divine with the jewellery of winter, or was veiled in living clouds; and I have heard her voice of winds, and snowy, tuneful waters when floods were falling; yet never did her soul reveal itself more impressively than now. I hung about her skirts, lingering timidly, until the higher mountains and glaciers compelled me to push up the canyon.

This canyon is accessible only to mountaineers, and I was anxious to carry my barometer and clinometer through it, to obtain sections and altitudes, so I chose it as the most attractive highway. After I had passed the tall groves that stretch a mile above Mirror Lake, and scrambled around the Tenaya Fall, which is just at the head of the lake groves, I crept through the dense and spiny chaparral that plushes the roots of the mountains here for miles in warm green, and was ascending a precipitous rock-front, smoothed by glacial action, when I suddenly fell – for the first time since I touched foot to Sierra rocks. After several somersaults, I became insensible from the shock, and when consciousness returned I found myself wedged among short, stiff bushes, trembling as if cold, not injured in the slightest.

Judging by the sun, I could not have been insensible very long; probably not a minute, possibly an hour; and I could not remember what made me fall, or where I had fallen from; but I saw that if I had rolled a little further, my mountain-climbing would have been finished, for just beyond the bushes the canyon wall steepened and I might have fallen to the bottom. 'There,' said I, addressing my feet, to whose separate skill I had learned to trust night and day on any mountain, 'that is what you get by intercourse with stupid town stairs, and dead pavements.' I felt degraded and worthless. I had not yet reached the most difficult portion of the canyon, but I determined to guide my humbled body over the most nerve-trying places I could find; for I was now awake, and felt confident that the last of the town fog had been shaken from both head and feet.

I camped at the mouth of a narrow gorge which is cut into the bottom of the main canyon, determined to take earnest exercise next day. No plushy boughs did my ill-behaved bones enjoy that night, nor did my bumped head get a spicy cedar plume pillow mixed with flowers. I slept on a naked boulder, and when I awoke all my nervous trembling was gone.

The gorged portion of the canyon, in which I spent all the next day, is about a mile and a half in length; and I passed the time in tracing the action of the forces that determined this peculiar bottom gorge, which is an abrupt, ragged-walled, narrow-throated canyon, formed in the bottom of the wide-mouthed, smooth, and bevelled main canyon. I will not stop now to tell you more; some day you may see it, like a shadowy line, from Cloud's Rest. In high water, the stream occupies all the bottom of the gorge, surging and chafing in glorious power from wall to wall. But the sound of the grinding was low as I entered the gorge, scarcely hoping to be able to pass through its entire length. By cool efforts, along glassy, ice-worn slopes, I reached the upper end in a little over a day, but was compelled to pass the second night in the gorge, and in the moonlight I wrote you this short pencil letter in my notebook:

> The moon is looking down into the canyon, and how marvellously the great rocks kindle to her light! Every dome, and brow, and swelling boss touched by her white rays, glows as if lighted with snow. I am now only a mile from last night's camp; and have been climbing and sketching all day in this difficult but instructive gorge. It is formed in the bottom of the main canyon, among the roots of Cloud's Rest. It begins at the filled-up lake-basin where I camped last night, and ends a few hundred yards above, in another basin of the same kind. The walls everywhere are craggy and vertical, and in some places they overlean. It is only from twenty to sixty feet wide, and not, though black and broken enough, the thin, crooked

mouth of some mysterious abyss; but it was eroded, for in many places I saw its solid, seamless floor.

I am sitting on a big stone, against which the stream divides, and goes brawling by in rapids on both sides; half of my rock is white in the light, half in shadow. As I look from the opening jaws of this shadowy gorge, South Dome is immediately in front – high in the stars, her face turned from the moon, with the rest of her body gloriously muffled in waved folds of granite. On the left, sculptured from the main Cloud's Rest ridge, are three magnificent rocks, sisters of the great South Dome. On the right is the massive, moonlit front of Mount Watkins, and between, low down in the furthest distance, is Sentinel Dome, girdled and darkened with forest. In the near foreground Tenaya Creek is singing against boulders that are white with snow and moonbeams. Now look back twenty yards, and you will see a waterfall fair as a spirit; the moonlight just touches it, bringing it into relief against a dark background of shadow. A little to the left, and a dozen steps this side of the fall, a flickering light marks my camp – and a precious camp it is. A huge, glacier-polished slab, falling from the smooth, glossy flank of Cloud's Rest, happened to settle on edge against the wall of the gorge. I did not know that this slab was glacier-polished until I lighted my fire. Judge of my delight. I think it was sent here by an earthquake. It is about twelve feet square. I wish I could take it home for a hearthstone. Beneath this slab is the only place in this torrent-swept gorge where I could find sand sufficient for a bed.

I expected to sleep on the boulders, for I spent most of the afternoon on the slippery wall of the canyon, endeavouring to get around this difficult part of the gorge, and was compelled to hasten down here for water before dark. I shall sleep soundly on this sand; half of it is mica. Here, wonderful to behold, are a few green stems of prickly rubus, and a tiny grass. They are here to meet us. Ay, even here in this darksome gorge, 'frightened and tormented' with raging torrents and choking avalanches of snow. Can it be? As if rubus and the grass leaf were not enough of God's tender prattle words of love, which we so much need in these mighty temples of power, yonder in the 'benmost bore' are two blessed adiantums. Listen to them! How wholly infused with God is this one big word of love that we call the world! Goodnight. Do you see the fire-glow on my ice-smoothed slab, and on my two ferns and the rubus and grass panicles? And do you hear how sweet a sleep-song the fall and cascades are singing?

The water-ground chips and knots that I found fastened between the rocks kept my fire alive all through the night. Next morning I rose nerved and ready for another day of sketching and noting, and any form of climbing. I escaped from the gorge about noon, after accomplishing some of the most delicate feats of mountaineering I ever attempted; and here the canyon is all broadly open again – the floor luxuriantly forested with pine, and spruce, and silver fir, and brown-trunked librocedrus. The walls rise in Yosemite forms, and Tenaya Creek comes down seven hundred feet in a white brush of foam. This is a little Yosemite valley. It is about two thousand feet above the level of the main Yosemite, and about 2400 below Lake Tenaya.

I found the lake frozen, and the ice was so clear and unruffled that the surrounding mountains and the groves that look down upon it were reflected almost as perfectly as I ever beheld them in the calm evening mirrors of summer. At a little distance, it was difficult to believe the lake frozen at all; and when I walked out on it, cautiously stamping at short intervals to test the strength of the ice, I seemed to walk mysteriously, without adequate faith, on the surface of the water. The ice was so transparent that I could see through it the beautifully wave-rippled, sandy bottom, and the scales of mica glinting back the down-pouring light. When I knelt down with my face close to the ice, through which the sun-beams were pouring, I was delighted to discover myriad of Tyndall's six-rayed water flowers, magnificently coloured.

A grand old mountain mansion is this Tenaya region! In the glacier period it was a *mer de glace*, far grander than the *mer de glace* of

Switzerland, which is only about half a mile broad. The Tenaya *mer de glace* was not less than two miles broad, late in the glacier epoch, when all the principal dividing crests were bare; and its depth was not less than 1500 feet. Ice-streams from Mounts Lyell and Dana, and all the mountains between, and from the nearer Cathedral Peak, flowed hither, welded into one, and worked together. After eroding this Tenaya Lake basin, and all the splendidly sculptured rocks and mountains that surround and adorn it, and the great Tenaya Canyon, with its wealth of all that makes mountains sublime, they were welded with the vast South, Lyell, and Illilouette glaciers on one side, and with those of Hoffman on the other – thus forming a portion of a yet grander *mer de glace* in Yosemite Valley.

I reached the Tenaya Canyon, on my way home, by coming in from the northeast, rambling down over the shoulders of Mount Watkins, touching bottom a mile above Mirror Lake. From thence home was but a saunter in the moonlight.

After resting one day, and the weather continuing calm, I ran up over the left shoulder of South Dome and down in front of its grand split face to make some measurements, completed my work, climbed to the right shoulder, struck off along the ridge for Cloud's Rest, and reached the topmost heave of her sunny wave in ample time to see the sunset.

Cloud's Rest is a thousand feet higher than Tissiack. It is a wavelike crest upon a ridge, which begins at Yosemite with Tissiack, and runs continuously eastward to the thicket of peaks and crests around Lake Tenaya. This lofty granite wall is bent this way and that by the restless and weariless action of glaciers just as if it had been made of dough. But the grand circumference of mountains and forests are coming from far and near, densing into one close assemblage; for the sun, their god and father, with love ineffable, is glowing a sunset farewell. Not one of all the assembled rocks or trees seemed remote. How impressively their faces shone with responsive love!

I ran home in the moonlight with firm strides; for the sun-love made me strong. Down through the junipers; down through the firs; now in jet shadows, now in white light; over sandy moraines and bare, clanking rocks; past the huge ghost of South Dome rising weird through the firs; past the glorious fall of Nevada, the groves of Illilouette; through the pines of the valley; beneath the bright crystal sky blazing with stars. All of this mountain wealth in one day! – one of the rich ripe days that enlarge one's life; so much of the sun upon one side of it, so much of the moon and stars on the other.

8

A PERILOUS NIGHT
ON SHASTA'S SUMMIT

John Muir

This essay merges two of Muir's Shasta adventures into one narrative. His first solo exploration of Shasta, during which he made his 'snow-camp', took place around 2nd November 1874. This story is fused with the near-death experience which Muir suffered with Jerome Fay on his third climb of Shasta on 30th April 1875. His second climb took place on 28th April, just two days earlier, when he led a geodetic survey party to the summit. The essay was first published in 1888 as part of a compilation entitled *Picturesque California* and was later included in *Steep Trails* by editor William Frederic Badè in 1918.

Toward the end of summer, after a light, open winter, one may reach the summit of Mount Shasta without passing over much snow, by keeping on the crest of a long narrow ridge, mostly bare, that extends from near the camp-ground at the timber-line. But on my first excursion to the summit the whole mountain, down to its low swelling base, was smoothly laden with loose fresh snow, presenting a most glorious mass of winter mountain scenery, in the midst of which I scrambled and revelled or lay snugly snowbound, enjoying the fertile clouds and the snow-bloom in all their growing, drifting grandeur.

I had walked from Redding, sauntering leisurely from station to station along the old Oregon stage road, the better to see the rocks and plants, birds and people, by the way, tracing the rushing Sacramento to its fountains around icy Shasta. The first rains had fallen on the lowlands, and the first snows on the mountains, and everything was fresh and bracing, while an abundance of balmy sunshine filled all the noonday hours. It was the calm afterglow that usually succeeds the first storm of the winter. I met many of the birds that had reared their young and spent their summer in the Shasta woods and chaparral. They were then on their way south to their winter homes, leading their young full-fledged and about as large and strong as the parents. Squirrels, dry and elastic after the storms, were busy about their stores of pine nuts, and the latest goldenrods were still in bloom, though it was now past the middle of October. The grand colour glow – the autumnal jubilee of ripe leaves – was past prime, but, freshened by the rain, was still making a fine show along the banks of the river and in the ravines and the dells of the smaller streams.

At the salmon-hatching establishment on the McCloud River I halted a week to examine the limestone belt, grandly developed there, to learn what I could of the inhabitants of the river and its banks, and to give time for the fresh snow that I knew had fallen on the mountain to settle somewhat, with a view to making the ascent. A pedestrian on these mountain roads, especially so late in the year, is sure to excite curiosity, and many were the interrogations concerning my ramble. When I said that I was simply taking a walk, and that icy Shasta was my mark, I was invariably admonished that I had come on a dangerous quest. The time was far too late, the snow was too loose and deep to climb, and I should be lost in drifts and slides. When I hinted that new snow was beautiful and storms not so bad as they were called, my advisers shook their heads in token of superior knowledge and declared the ascent of 'Shasta Butte' through loose snow impossible. Nevertheless, before noon of the second of November I was in the frosty azure of the utmost summit.

When I arrived at Sisson's everything was quiet. The last of the summer visitors had flitted long before, and the deer and bears also were beginning to seek their winter homes. My barometer and the sighing winds and filmy, half-transparent clouds that dimmed the sunshine gave notice of the approach of another storm, and I was in haste to be off and get myself established somewhere in the midst of it, whether the summit was to be attained or not. Sisson, who is a mountaineer, speedily fitted me out for storm or calm as only a mountaineer could, with warm blankets and a week's provisions so generous in quantity and kind that they easily might have been made to last a month in case of my being closely snowbound. Well I knew the weariness of snow-climbing, and the frosts, and the dangers of mountaineering so late in the year; therefore I could not ask a guide to go with me, even had one been willing. All I wanted was to have blankets and provisions deposited as far up in the timber as the snow would permit a pack-animal to go. There I could build a storm nest and lie warm, and make raids up and around the mountain in accordance with the weather.

Setting out on the afternoon of November first, with Jerome Fay, mountaineer and guide, in charge of the animals, I was soon plodding wearily upward through the muffled winter woods, the snow of course growing steadily deeper and looser, so that we had to break a trail. The animals began to get discouraged, and after night and darkness came on they became entangled in a bed of rough lava, where, breaking through four or five feet of mealy snow, their feet were caught between angular boulders. Here they were in danger of being lost, but after we had removed packs and saddles and assisted their efforts with ropes, they all escaped to the side of a ridge about a 1000 feet below the timber-line.

To go farther was out of the question, so we were compelled to camp as best we could. A pitch-pine fire speedily changed the temperature and shed a blaze of light on the wild lava-slope and the straggling storm-bent pines around us. Melted snow answered for coffee, and we had plenty of venison to roast. Toward midnight I rolled myself in my blankets, slept an hour and a half, arose and ate more venison, tied two days' provisions to my belt, and set out for the summit, hoping to reach it ere the coming storm should fall. Jerome accompanied me a little distance above camp and indicated the way as well as he could in the darkness. He seemed loath to leave me, but, being reassured that I was at home and required no care, he bade me goodbye and returned to camp, ready to lead his animals down the mountain at daybreak.

After I was above the dwarf pines, it was fine practice pushing up the broad unbroken slopes of snow, alone in the solemn silence of the night. Half the sky was clouded; in the other half the stars sparkled icily in the keen, frosty air; while everywhere the glorious wealth of snow fell away from the summit of the cone in flowing folds, more extensive and continuous than any I had ever seen before. When day dawned the clouds were crawling slowly and becoming more massive, but gave no intimation of immediate danger, and I pushed on faithfully, though holding myself well in hand, ready to return to the timber; for it was easy to see that the storm was not far off. The mountain rises 10,000 feet above the general level of the country, in blank exposure to the deep upper currents of the sky, and no labyrinth of peaks and canyons I had ever been in seemed to me so dangerous as these immense slopes, bare against the sky.

The frost was intense, and drifting snow-dust made breathing at times rather difficult. The snow was as dry as meal, and the finer particles drifted freely, rising high in the air, while the larger portions of the crystals rolled like sand. I frequently sank to my armpits between buried blocks of loose lava, but generally only to my knees. When tired with walking I still wallowed slowly upward on all fours. The steepness of the slope – thirty-five degrees in some places – made any kind of progress fatiguing, while small avalanches were being constantly set in motion in the steepest places. But the bracing air and the sublime beauty of the snowy expanse thrilled every nerve and made absolute exhaustion impossible. I seemed to be walking and wallowing in a cloud; but, holding steadily onward, by half-past ten o'clock I had gained the highest summit.

I held my commanding foothold in the sky for two hours, gazing on the glorious landscapes spread map-like around the immense horizon, and tracing the outlines of the ancient lava-streams extending far into the surrounding plains, and the pathways of vanished glaciers of which Shasta had been the centre. But, as I had left my coat in camp for the sake of having my limbs free in climbing, I soon was cold. The wind increased in violence, raising the snow in magnificent drifts that were drawn out in the form of wavering banners glowing in the sun. Toward the end of my stay a succession of small clouds struck against the summit rocks like drifting icebergs, darkening the air as they passed, and producing a chill as definite and sudden as if ice-water had been dashed in my face. This is the kind of cloud in which snow-flowers grow, and I turned and fled.

Finding that I was not closely pursued, I ventured to take time on the way down for a visit to the head of the Whitney Glacier and the 'Crater Butte'. After I reached the end of the main summit ridge the descent was but little more than one continuous soft, mealy, muffled slide, most luxurious and rapid, though the hissing, swishing speed attained was obscured in great part by flying snow-dust – a marked contrast to the boring seal-wallowing upward struggle. I reached camp about an hour before dusk, hollowed a strip of loose ground in the lee of a large block of red lava, where firewood was abundant, rolled myself in my blankets, and went to sleep.

Next morning, having slept little the night before the ascent and being weary with climbing after the excitement was over, I slept late. Then, awaking suddenly, my eyes opened on one of the most beautiful and sublime scenes I ever enjoyed. A boundless wilderness of storm-clouds of different degrees of ripeness were congregated over all the lower landscape for thousands of square miles, coloured grey, and purple, and pearl, and deep-glowing white, amid which I seemed to be floating; while the great white cone of the mountain above was all aglow in the free, blazing sunshine. It seemed not so much an ocean as a *land* of clouds – undulating hill and dale, smooth purple plains, and silvery mountains of cumuli, range over range, diversified with peak and dome and hollow fully brought out in light and shade.

I gazed enchanted, but cold grey masses, drifting like dust on a wind-swept plain, began to shut out the light, forerunners of the coming storm I had been so anxiously watching. I made haste to gather as much wood as possible, snugging it as a shelter around my bed. The storm side of my blankets was fastened down with stakes to reduce as much as possible the sifting-in of drift and the danger of being blown away. The precious bread-sack was placed safely as a pillow, and when at length the first flakes fell I was exultingly ready to welcome them. Most of my firewood was more than half rosin and would blaze in the face of the fiercest drifting; the winds could not demolish my bed, and my bread could be made to last indefinitely; while in case of need I had the means of making snowshoes and could retreat or hold my ground as I pleased.

Presently the storm broke forth into full snowy bloom, and the thronging crystals darkened the air. The wind swept past in hissing floods, grinding the snow into meal and sweeping down into the hollows in enormous drifts all the heavier particles, while the finer dust was sifted through the sky, increasing the icy gloom. But my fire glowed bravely as if in glad defiance of the drift to quench it, and, notwithstanding but little trace of my nest could be seen after the snow had levelled and buried it, I was snug and warm, and the passionate uproar produced a glad excitement.

Day after day the storm continued, piling snow on snow in weariless abundance. There were short periods of quiet, when the sun would seem to look eagerly down through rents in the clouds, as if to know how the work was advancing. During these calm intervals I replenished my fire – sometimes without leaving the nest, for fire and woodpile were so near this could easily be done – or busied myself with my notebook, watching the gestures of the trees in taking the snow, examining separate crystals under a lens, and learning the methods of their deposition as an enduring fountain for the streams. Several times, when the storm ceased for a few minutes, a Douglas squirrel came frisking from the foot of a clump of dwarf pines, moving in sudden interrupted spurts over the bossy snow; then, without any apparent guidance, he would dig rapidly into the drift where were buried some grains of barley that the horses had left. The Douglas squirrel does not strictly belong to these upper woods, and I was surprised to see him out in such weather. The mountain sheep also, quite a large flock of them, came to my camp and took shelter beside a clump of matted dwarf pines a little above my nest.

The storm lasted about a week, but before it was ended Sisson became alarmed and sent up the guide with animals to see what had become of me and recover the camp outfit. The news spread that 'there was a man on the mountain', and he must surely have perished, and Sisson was blamed for allowing any one to attempt climbing in such weather; while I was as safe as anybody in the lowlands, lying like a squirrel in a warm fluffy nest, busied about my own affairs and wishing only to be let alone. Later, however, a trail could not have been broken for a horse, and some of the camp furniture would have had to be abandoned. On the fifth day I returned to Sisson's, and from that comfortable base made excursions, as the weather permitted, to the foot of the Whitney Glacier, around the base of the mountain, to Rhett and Klamath Lakes, to the Modoc region and elsewhere, developing many interesting scenes and experiences.

But the next spring, on the other side of this eventful winter, I saw and felt still more of the Shasta snow. For then it was my fortune to get into the very heart of a Shasta storm and to be held in it for a long time.

On the 28th of April [1875] I led a party up the mountain for the purpose of making a survey of the summit with reference to the location of the Geodetic monument. On the 30th, accompanied by Jerome Fay, I made another ascent to make some barometrical observations, the day intervening between the two ascents being devoted to establishing a camp on the extreme edge of the timber line. Here, on our red trachyte bed, we obtained two hours of shallow sleep broken for occasional glimpses of the keen, starry night. At two o'clock we rose, breakfasted on a warmed tin-cupful of coffee and a piece of frozen venison broiled on the coals, and started for the summit. Up to this time there was nothing in sight that betokened the approach of a storm; but on gaining the summit, we saw toward Lassen's Butte hundreds of square miles of white cumuli boiling dreamily in the sunshine far beneath us, and causing no alarm.

The slight weariness of the ascent was soon rested away, and our glorious morning in the sky promised nothing but enjoyment. At 9 a.m. the dry thermometer stood at 34° in the shade and rose steadily until at 1 p.m. it stood at 50°, probably influenced somewhat by radiation from the sun-warmed cliffs. A common bumblebee, not at all benumbed, zigzagged vigorously about our heads for a few moments, as if unconscious of the fact that the nearest honey flower was a mile beneath him.

In the meantime clouds were growing down in Shasta Valley – massive swelling cumuli, displaying delicious tones of purple and grey in the hollows of their sun-beaten bosses. Extending gradually southward around on both sides of Shasta, these at length united with the older field towards Lassen's Butte, thus encircling Mount Shasta in one continuous cloud-zone. Rhett and Klamath Lakes were eclipsed beneath clouds scarcely less brilliant than their own silvery disks. The Modoc Lava Beds, many a snow-laden peak far north in Oregon, the Scott and Trinity and Siskiyou Mountains, the peaks of the Sierra, the blue Coast Range, Shasta Valley, the dark forests filling the valley of the Sacramento, all in turn were obscured or buried, leaving the lofty cone on which we stood solitary in the sunshine between two skies – a sky of spotless blue above, a sky of glittering cloud beneath. The creative sun shone glorious on the vast expanse of cloudland; hill and dale, mountain and valley springing into existence responsive to his rays and steadily developing in beauty and individuality. One huge mountain-cone of cloud, corresponding to Mount Shasta in these newborn cloud-ranges, rose close alongside with a visible motion, its firm, polished bosses seeming so near and substantial that we almost fancied we might leap down upon them from where we stood and make our way to the lowlands. No hint was given, by anything in their appearance, of the fleeting character of these most sublime and beautiful cloud mountains. On the contrary they impressed one as being lasting additions to the landscape.

The weather of the springtime and summer, throughout the Sierra in general, is usually varied by slight local rains and dustings of snow, most of which are obviously far too joyous and life-giving to be regarded as storms – single clouds growing in the sunny sky, ripening in an hour, showering the heated landscape, and passing away like a thought, leaving no visible bodily remains to stain the sky. Snow-storms of the same gentle kind abound among the high peaks, but in spring they not unfrequently attain larger proportions, assuming a violence and energy of expression scarcely surpassed by those bred in the depths of winter. Such was the storm now gathering about us.

It began to declare itself shortly after noon, suggesting to us the idea of at once seeking our safe camp in the timber and abandoning the purpose of making an observation of the barometer at 3 p.m., – two having already been made, at 9 a.m., and 12 noon, while simultaneous observations were made at Strawberry Valley. Jerome peered at short intervals over the ridge, contemplating the rising clouds with anxious gestures in the rough wind, and at length declared that if we did not make a speedy escape we should be compelled to pass the rest of the day and night on the summit. But anxiety to complete my observations stifled my own instinctive promptings to retreat, and held me to my work. No inexperienced person was depending on me, and I told Jerome that we two mountaineers should be able to make our way down through any storm likely to fall.

Presently thin, fibrous films of cloud began to blow directly over the summit from north to south, drawn out in long fairy webs like carded wool, forming and dissolving as if by magic. The wind twisted them into ringlets and whirled them in a succession of graceful convolutions like the outside sprays of Yosemite Falls in flood-time; then, sailing out into the thin azure over the precipitous brink of the ridge they were drifted together like wreaths of foam on a river. These higher and finer cloud fabrics were evidently produced by the chilling of the air from its own expansion caused by the upward deflection of the wind against the slopes of the mountain. They steadily increased on the north rim of the cone, forming at length a thick, opaque, ill-defined embankment from the icy meshes of which snow-flowers began to fall, alternating with hail. The sky speedily darkened, and just as I had completed my last observation and boxed my instruments ready for the descent, the storm began in serious earnest. At first the cliffs were beaten with hail, every stone of which, as far as I could see, was regular in form, six-sided pyramids with rounded base, rich and sumptuous looking, and fashioned with loving care, yet seemingly thrown away on those desolate crags down which they went rolling, falling, sliding in a network of curious streams.

After we had forced our way down the ridge and past the group of hissing fumaroles, the storm became inconceivably violent. The thermometer fell 22° in a few minutes, and soon dropped below zero. The hail gave place to snow, and darkness came on like night. The wind, rising to the highest pitch of violence, boomed and surged amid the desolate crags; lightning-flashes in quick succession cut the gloomy darkness; and the thunders, the most tremendously loud and appalling I ever heard, made an almost continuous roar, stroke following stroke in quick, passionate succession, as though the mountain were being rent to its foundations and the fires of the old volcano were breaking forth again.

Could we at once have begun to descend the snow-slopes leading to the timber, we might have made good our escape, however dark and wild the storm. As it was, we had first to make our way along a dangerous ridge nearly a mile and a half long, flanked in many places by steep ice-slopes at the head of the Whitney Glacier on one side and by shattered precipices on the other. Apprehensive of this coming darkness, I had taken the precaution, when the storm began, to make the most dangerous points clear to my mind, and to mark their relations with reference to the direction of the wind. When, therefore, the darkness came on, and the bewildering drift, I felt confident that we could force our way through it with no other guidance. After passing the 'Hot Springs' I halted in the lee of a lava-block to let Jerome, who had fallen a little behind, come up. Here he opened a council in which, under circumstances sufficiently exciting but without evincing any bewilderment, he maintained, in opposition to my views, that it was impossible to proceed. He firmly refused to make the venture to find the camp, while I, aware of the dangers that would necessarily attend our efforts, and conscious of being the cause of his present peril, decided not to leave him.

Our discussions ended, Jerome made a dash from the shelter of the lava-block and began forcing his way back against the wind to the 'Hot Springs', wavering and struggling to resist being carried away, as if he were fording a rapid stream. After waiting and watching in vain for some flaw in the storm that might be urged as a new argument in favour of attempting the descent, I was compelled to follow. 'Here,' said Jerome, as we shivered in the midst of the hissing, sputtering fumaroles, 'we shall be safe from frost.'

'Yes,' said I, 'we can lie in this mud and steam and sludge, warm at least on one side; but how can we protect our lungs from the acid gases, and how, after our clothing is saturated, shall we be able to reach camp without freezing, even after the storm is over? We shall have to wait for sunshine, and when will it come?'

The tempered area to which we had committed ourselves extended over about one fourth of an acre; but it was only about an eighth of an inch in thickness, for the scalding gas-jets were shorn off close to the ground by the oversweeping flood of frosty wind. And how lavishly the snow fell only mountaineers may know. The crisp crystal flowers seemed to touch one another and fairly to thicken the tremendous blast that carried them. This was the bloom-time, the summer of the cloud, and never before have I seen even a mountain cloud flowering so profusely.

When the bloom of the Shasta chaparral is falling, the ground is sometimes covered for hundreds of square miles to a depth of half an inch. But the bloom of this fertile snow-cloud grew and matured and fell to a depth of two feet in a few hours. Some crystals landed with their rays almost perfect, but most of them were worn and broken by striking against one another, or by rolling on the ground. The touch of these snow-flowers in calm weather is infinitely gentle – glinting, swaying, settling silently in the dry mountain air, or massed in flakes soft and downy. To lie out alone in the mountains of a still night and be touched by the first of these small silent messengers from the sky is a memorable experience, and the fineness of that touch none will forget. But the storm-blast laden with crisp, sharp snow seems to crush and bruise and stupefy with its multitude of stings, and compels the bravest to turn and flee.

The snow fell without abatement until an hour or two after what seemed to be the natural darkness of the night. Up to the time the storm first broke on the summit its development was remarkably gentle. There was a deliberate growth of clouds, a weaving of translucent tissue above, then the roar of the wind and the thunder, and the darkening flight of snow. Its subsidence was not less sudden. The clouds broke and vanished, not a crystal was left in the sky, and the stars shone out with pure and tranquil radiance.

During the storm we lay on our backs so as to present as little surface as possible to the wind, and to let the drift pass over us. The mealy snow sifted into the folds of our clothing and in many places reached the skin. We were glad at first to see the snow packing about us, hoping it would deaden the force of the wind, but it soon froze into a stiff, crusty heap as the temperature fell, rather augmenting our novel misery.

When the heat became unendurable, on some spot where steam was escaping through the sludge, we tried to stop it with snow and mud, or shifted a little at a time by shoving with our heels; for to stand in blank exposure to the fearful wind in our frozen-and-broiled condition seemed certain death. The acrid incrustations sublimed from the escaping gases frequently gave way, opening new vents to scald us; and, fearing that if at any time the wind should fall, carbonic acid, which often formed a considerable portion of the gaseous exhalations of volcanoes, might collect in sufficient quantities to cause sleep and death, I warned Jerome against forgetting himself for a single moment, even should his sufferings admit of such a thing.

Accordingly, when during the long, dreary watches of the night we roused from a state of half-consciousness, we called each other by name in a frightened, startled way, each fearing the other might be benumbed or dead. The ordinary sensations of cold give but a faint conception of that which comes on after hard climbing with want of food and sleep in such exposure as this. Life is then seen to be a fire, that now smoulders, now brightens, and may be easily quenched. The weary hours wore away like dim half-forgotten years, so long and eventful they seemed, though we did nothing but suffer. Still the pain was not always of that bitter, intense kind that precludes thought and takes away all capacity for enjoyment. A sort of dreamy stupor came on at times in which we fancied we saw dry, resinous logs suitable for campfires, just as after going days without food men fancy they see bread.

Frozen, blistered, famished, benumbed, our bodies seemed lost to us at times – all dead but the eyes. For the duller and fainter we became the clearer was our vision, though only in momentary glimpses. Then, after the sky cleared, we gazed at the stars, blessed immortals of light, shining with marvellous brightness with long lance rays, near-looking and new-looking, as if never seen before. Again they would look familiar and remind us of star-gazing at home. Oftentimes imagination coming into play would present charming pictures of the warm zone below, mingled with others near and far. Then the bitter wind and the drift would break the blissful vision and dreary pains cover us like clouds. 'Are you suffering much?' Jerome would inquire with pitiful faintness.

'Yes,' I would say, striving to keep my voice brave, 'frozen and burned; but never mind, Jerome, the night will wear away at last, and tomorrow we go a-Maying, and what campfires we will make, and what sun-baths we will take!'

The frost grew more and more intense, and we became icy and covered over with a crust of frozen snow, as if we had lain cast away in the drift all winter. In about thirteen hours – every hour like a year – day began to dawn, but it was long ere the summit's rocks were touched by the sun. No clouds were visible from where we lay, yet the morning was dull and blue, and bitterly frosty; and hour after hour passed by while we eagerly watched the pale light stealing down the ridge to the hollow where we lay. But there was not a trace of that warm, flushing sunrise splendour we so long had hoped for.

As the time drew near to make an effort to reach camp, we became concerned to know what strength was left us, and whether or no we could walk; for we had lain flat all this time without once rising to our feet. Mountaineers, however, always find in themselves a reserve of power after great exhaustion. It is a kind of second life, available only in emergencies like this; and, having proved its existence, I had no great fear that either of us would fail, though one of my arms was already benumbed and hung powerless.

At length, after the temperature was somewhat mitigated on this memorable first of May, we arose and began to struggle homeward. Our frozen trousers could scarcely be made to bend at the knee, and we waded the snow with difficulty. The summit ridge was fortunately wind-swept and nearly bare, so we were not compelled to lift our feet high, and on reaching the long home slopes laden with loose snow we made rapid progress, sliding and shuffling and pitching headlong, our feebleness accelerating rather than diminishing our speed. When we had descended some 3000 feet the sunshine warmed our backs and we began to revive. At 10 a.m. we reached the timber and were safe.

Half an hour later we heard Sisson shouting down among the firs, coming with horses to take us to the hotel. After breaking a trail through the snow as far as possible he had tied his animals and walked up. We had been so long without food that we cared but little about eating, but we eagerly drank the coffee he prepared for us. Our feet were frozen, and thawing them was painful, and had to be done very slowly by keeping them buried in soft snow for several hours, which avoided permanent damage. Five thousand feet below the summit we found only three inches of new snow, and at the base of the mountain only a slight shower of rain had fallen, showing how local our storm had been, notwithstanding its terrific fury. Our feet were wrapped in sacking, and we were soon mounted and on our way down into the thick sunshine – 'God's Country', as Sisson calls the Chaparral Zone. In two hours' ride the last snow-bank was left behind. Violets appeared along the edges of the trail, and the chaparral was coming into bloom, with young lilies and larkspurs about the open places in rich profusion. How beautiful seemed the golden sunbeams streaming through the woods between the warm brown boles of the cedars and pines! All my friends among the birds and plants seemed like *old* friends, and we felt like speaking to every one of them as we passed, as if we had been a long time away in some far, strange country.

In the afternoon we reached Strawberry Valley and fell asleep. Next morning we seemed to have risen from the dead. My bedroom was flooded with sunshine, and from the window I saw the great white Shasta cone clad in forests and clouds and bearing them loftily in the sky. Everything seemed full and radiant with the freshness and beauty and enthusiasm of youth. Sisson's children came in with flowers and covered my bed, and the storm on the mountain-top vanished like a dream.

9

THE SOUTH DOME

John Muir

This is Muir's account of the second ascent of South Dome which he
made on 10th November 1875 following the bolted route which
George Anderson had pioneered earlier that year. It was published in
The Mountains of California, 1894.

With the exception of a few spires and pinnacles, the South Dome is
the only rock about the Valley that is strictly inaccessible without
artificial means, and its inaccessibility is expressed in severe terms.
Nevertheless many a mountaineer, gazing admiringly, tried hard to
invent a way to the top of its noble crown – all in vain, until in the
year 1875, George Anderson, an indomitable Scotchman, undertook
the adventure.

The side facing Tenaya Canyon is an absolutely vertical precipice
from the summit to a depth of about 1600 feet, and on the opposite
side it is nearly vertical for about as great a depth. The southwest side
presents a very steep and finely drawn curve from the top down 1000
feet or more, while on the northeast, where it is united with the
Clouds' Rest Ridge, one may easily reach a point called the Saddle,
about 700 feet below the summit. From the Saddle the Dome rises in
a graceful curve a few degrees too steep for unaided climbing, besides
being defended by overleaning ends of the concentric dome layers of
the granite.

A year or two before Anderson gained the summit, John Conway,
the master trail-builder of the Valley, and his little sons, who
climbed smooth rocks like lizards, made a bold effort to reach
the top by climbing barefooted up the grand curve with a rope
which they fastened at irregular intervals by means of eye-bolts
driven into joints of the rock. But finding that the upper part would

require laborious drilling, they abandoned the attempt, glad to escape from the dangerous position they had reached, some 300 feet above the Saddle. Anderson began with Conway's old rope, which had been left in place, and resolutely drilled his way to the top, inserting eyebolts five to six feet apart, and making his rope fast to each in succession, resting his feet on the last bolt while he drilled a hole for the next above. Occasionally some irregularity in the curve, or slight foothold, would enable him to climb a few feet without a rope, which he would pass and begin drilling again, and thus the whole work was accomplished in a few days. From this slender beginning he proposed to construct a substantial stairway which he hoped to complete in time for the next year's travel, but while busy getting out timber for his stairway and dreaming of the wealth he hoped to gain from tolls, he was taken sick and died all alone in his little cabin.

On the 10th of November, after returning from a visit to Mount Shasta, a month or two after Anderson had gained the summit, I made haste to the Dome, not only for the pleasure of climbing, but to see what I might learn. The first winter storm clouds had blossomed and the mountains and all the high points about the Valley were mantled in fresh snow. I was, therefore, a little apprehensive of danger from the slipperiness of the rope and the rock. Anderson himself tried to prevent me from making the attempt, refusing to believe that anyone could climb his rope in the snow-muffled condition in which it then was. Moreover, the sky was overcast and solemn snow clouds began to curl around the summit, and my late experiences on icy Shasta came to mind. But reflecting that I had matches in my pocket, and that I might find a little firewood, I concluded that in case of a storm the night could be spent on the Dome without any suffering worth minding, no matter what the clouds might bring forth. I therefore pushed on and gained the top.

It was one of those brooding, changeful days that come between the Indian summer and winter, when the leaf colours have grown dim and the clouds come and go among the cliffs like living creatures looking for work: now hovering aloft, now caressing rugged rock brows with great gentleness, or, wandering afar over the tops of the forests, touching the spires of fir and pine with their soft silken fringes as if trying to tell the glad news of the coming of snow.

The first view was perfectly glorious. A massive cloud of pure pearl lustre, apparently as fixed and calm as the meadows and groves in the shadow beneath it, was arched across the Valley from wall to wall, one end resting on the grand abutment of El Capitan, the other on Cathedral Rock. A little later, as I stood on the tremendous verge overlooking Mirror Lake, a flock of smaller clouds, white as snow, came from the north, trailing their downy skirts over the dark forests, and entered the Valley with solemn god-like gestures through Indian Canyon and over the North Dome and Royal Arches, moving swiftly, yet with majestic deliberation. On they came, nearer and nearer, gathering and massing beneath my feet and filling the Tenaya Canyon. Then the sun shone free, lighting the pearly grey surface of the cloud-like sea and making it glow. Gazing, admiring, I was startled to see for the first time the rare optical phenomenon of the 'Spectre of the Brocken'. My shadow, clearly outlined, about half a mile long, lay upon this glorious white surface with startling effect. I walked back and forth, waved my arms and struck all sorts of attitudes, to see every slightest movement enormously exaggerated. Considering that I have looked down so many times from mountain-tops on seas of all sorts of clouds, it seems strange that I should have seen the "Brocken Spectre" only this once. A grander surface and a grander standpoint, however, could hardly have been found in all the Sierra.

After this grand show the cloud sea rose higher, wreathing the Dome and submerging it for a short time, making darkness like night, and I began to think of looking for a camp-ground in a cluster of dwarf pines. But soon the sun shone free again, the clouds, sinking lower and lower, gradually vanished, leaving the Valley with its Indian-summer colours apparently refreshed, while to the eastward the summit peaks, clad in new snow, towered along the horizon in glorious array.

Though apparently it is perfectly bald, there are four clumps of pines growing on the summit representing three species, *Pinus albicaulis, P. contorta* and *P. ponderosa,* var. *Jeffreyi* – all three, of course, repressed and storm-beaten. The alpine spiræa grows here also and blossoms profusely with potentilla, erigeron, eriogonum, pent-stemon, solidago, an interesting species of onion, and four or five of grasses and sedges. None of these differs in any respect from those of other summits of the same height, excepting the curious little narrow-leaved, waxen-bulbed onion, which I had not seen elsewhere.

Notwithstanding the enthusiastic eagerness of tourists to reach the crown of the Dome, the views of the Valley from this lofty standpoint are less striking than from many other points comparatively low, chiefly on account of the foreshortening effect produced by looking down from so great a height. The North Dome is dwarfed almost beyond recognition, the grand sculpture of the Royal Arches is scarcely noticeable, and the whole range of walls on both sides seem comparatively low, especially when the Valley is flooded with noon sunshine; while the Dome itself, the most sublime feature of all the Yosemite views, is out of sight beneath one's feet. The view of Little Yosemite Valley is very fine, though inferior to one obtained from the base of the Starr King Cone, but the summit landscapes toward Mounts Ritter, Lyell, Dana, Conness, and the Merced group, are very effective and complete.

No one has attempted to carry out Anderson's plan of making the Dome accessible. For my part I should prefer leaving it in pure wildness, though, after all, no great damage could be done by tramping over it. The surface would be strewn with tin cans and bottles, but the winter gales would blow the rubbish away. Ava-lanches might strip off any sort of stairway or ladder that might be built. Blue jays and Clark crows have trodden the Dome for many a day, and so have beetles and chipmunks, and Tissiack would hardly be more "conquered" or spoiled should man be added to her list of visitors. His louder scream and heavier scrambling would not stir a line of her countenance.

When the sublime ice floods of the glacial period poured down the flank of the range over what is now Yosemite Valley, they were compelled to break through a dam of domes extending across from Mount Starr King to North Dome; and as the period began to draw near a close the shallowing ice currents were divided and the South Dome was, perhaps, the first to emerge, burnished and shining like a mirror above the surface of the icy sea; and though it has sustained the wear and tear of the elements tens of thousands of years, it yet remains a telling monument of the action of the great glaciers that brought it to light. Its entire surface is still covered with glacial hieroglyphics whose interpretation is the reward of all who devoutly study them.

10

THE RESCUE
ON GLENORA PEAK

Samuel Hall Young

From *Alaska Days with John Muir*. This is Young's description of the
climb he and John Muir made in 1879 of 8000-foot Glenora Peak in
Alaska (now in British Columbia), and of the accident which nearly
cost his life.

In the summer of 1879 I was stationed at Fort Wrangell in southeastern Alaska, whence I had come the year before, a green young
student fresh from college and seminary very – green and very fresh –
to do what I could towards establishing the white man's civilisation
among the Thlinget Indians. I had very many things to learn and
many more to unlearn.

Thither came by the monthly mail steamboat in July to aid and
counsel me in my work three men of national reputation – Dr Henry
Kendall of New York; Dr Aaron L Lindsley of Portland, Oregon, and
Dr Sheldon Jackson of Denver and the West. Their wives accompanied them and they were to spend a month with us.

Standing a little apart from them as the steamboat drew to the
dock, his peering blue eyes already eagerly scanning the islands and
mountains, was a lean, sinewy man of forty, with waving, reddish-
brown hair and beard, and shoulders slightly stooped. He wore a
Scotch cap and a long, grey tweed Ulster, which I have always since
associated with him, and which seemed the same garment, unsoiled
and unchanged, that he wore later on his northern trips. He was
introduced as Professor Muir, the Naturalist. A hearty grip of the
hand, and we seemed to coalesce at once in a friendship which, to me
at least, has been one of the very best things I have known in a life full
of blessings. From the first he was the strongest and most attractive of

114

these four fine personalities to me, and I began to recognise him as my Master who was to lead me into enchanting regions of beauty and mystery, which without his aid must forever have remained unseen by the eyes of my soul. I sat at his feet; and at the feet of his spirit I still sit, a student, absorbed, surrendered, as this 'priest of Nature's inmost shrine' unfolds to me the secrets of his 'mountains of God'.

Minor excursions culminated in the chartering of the little steamer *Cassiar*, on which our party, augmented by two or three friends, steamed between the tremendous glaciers and through the columned canyons of the swift Stickeen River through the narrow strip of Alaska's cup-handle to Glenora, in British Columbia, 150 miles from the river's mouth. Our captain was Nat Lane, a grandson of the famous Senator Joseph Lane of Oregon. Stocky, broad-shouldered, muscular, given somewhat to strange oaths and strong liquids, and eyeing askance our group as we struck the bargain, he was withal a genial, good-natured man, and a splendid river pilot.

Dropping down from Telegraph Creek we tied up at Glenora about noon of a cloudless day. 'Amuse yourselves,' said Captain Lane at lunch. 'Here we stay till two o'clock tomorrow morning. This gale, blowing from the sea, makes safe steering through the Canyon impossible, unless we take the morning's calm.' I saw Muir's eyes light up with a peculiar meaning as he glanced quickly at me across the table. He knew the leading strings I was in; how those well-meaning Doctors of Divinity (D.D.s) and their motherly wives thought they had a special mission to suppress all my self-destructive proclivities toward dangerous adventure, and especially to protect me from 'that wild Muir' and his hare-brained schemes of mountain climbing.

'Where is it?' I asked, as we met behind the pilot house a moment later.

He pointed to a little group of jagged peaks rising right up from where we stood – a pulpit in the centre of a vast rotunda of magnificent mountains.

'One of the finest viewpoints in the world,' he said.

'How far to the highest point?'

'About ten miles.'

'How high?'

'Seven or eight thousand feet.'

That was enough. I caught the D.D.s with guile. There were Stickeen Indians there catching salmon, and among them Chief Shakes, who our interpreter said was 'The youngest but the headest Chief of all.' Last night's palaver had whetted the appetites of both sides for more. On the part of the Indians, a talk with these 'Great White Chiefs from Washington' offered unlimited possibilities for material favour; and to the good divines the 'simple faith and childlike docility' of these children of the forest were a constant delight. And then how well their high-flown compliments and flowery metaphors would sound in article and speech to the wondering East! So I sent Stickeen Johnny, the interpreter, to call the natives to another *hyon wawa* (big talk) and, notebook in hand, the doctors 'went gayly to the fray'. I set the speeches a-going, and then slipped out to join the impatient Muir.

'Take off your coat,' he commanded, 'and here's your supper.'

Pocketing two hardtacks apiece we were off, keeping in shelter of house and bush till out of sight of the council-house and the flower-picking ladies. Then we broke out. What a matchless climate! What sweet, lung-filling air! Sunshine that had no weakness in it – as if we were springing plants. Our sinews like steel springs, muscles like India rubber, feet soled with iron to grip the rocks. Ten miles? Eight thousand feet? Why, I felt equal to forty miles and the Matterhorn!

'Eh, mon!' said Muir, lapsing into the broad Scotch he was so fond of using when enjoying himself, 'ye'll see the sicht o' yer life the day. Ye'll get that'll be o' mair use till ye than a' the gowd o' Cassiar.'

From the first, it was a hard climb. Fallen timber at the mountain's foot covered with thick brush swallowed us up and plucked us back. Beyond, on the steeper slopes, grew dwarf evergreens, five or six feet high – the same fir that towers a hundred feet with a diameter of three or four on the river banks, but here stunted by icy mountain winds. The curious blasting of the branches on the side next to the mountain gave them the appearance of long-armed, humpbacked, hairy gnomes, bristling with anger, stretching forbidding arms downwards to bar our passage to their sacred heights. Sometimes an inviting vista through the branches would lure us in, when it would narrow, and at its upper angle we would find a solid phalanx of these grumpy dwarfs.

Then we had to attack boldly, scrambling over the obstinate, elastic arms and against the clusters of stiff needles, till we gained the upper side and found another green slope.

Muir led, of course, picking with sure instinct the easiest way. Three hours of steady work brought us suddenly beyond the timber-line, and the real joy of the day began. Nowhere else have I seen anything approaching the luxuriance and variety of delicate blossoms shown by these high, mountain pastures of the North. 'You scarce could see the grass for flowers.' Everything that was marvellous in form, fair in colour, or sweet in fragrance seemed to be represented there, from daisies and campanulas to Muir's favourite, the cassiope, with its exquisite little pink-white bells shaped like lilies-of-the-valley and its subtle perfume. Muir at once went wild when we reached this fairyland. From cluster to cluster of flowers he ran, falling on his knees, babbling in unknown tongues, prattling a curious mixture of scientific lingo and baby talk, worshipping his little blue-and-pink goddesses.

'Ah! my blue-eyed darlin', little did I think to see you here. How did you stray away from Shasta?'

'Well, well! Who'd 'a' thought that you'd have left that niche in the Merced mountains to come here!'

'And who might you be, now, with your wonder look? Is it possible that you can be (two Latin polysyllables)? You're lost, my dear; you belong in Tennessee.'

'Ah! I thought I'd find you, my homely little sweetheart,' and so on unceasingly.

So absorbed was he in this amatory botany that he seemed to forget my existence. While I, as glad as he, tagged along, running up and down with him, asking now and then a question, learning something of plant life, but far more of that spiritual insight into Nature's lore which is granted only to those who love and woo her in her great outdoor palaces. But how I anathematised my short-sighted foolishness for having as a student at old Wooster shirked botany for the 'more important' studies of language and metaphysics. For here was a man whose natural science had a thorough technical basis, while the superstructure was built of 'lively stones', and was itself a living temple of love!

With all his boyish enthusiasm, Muir was a most painstaking student; and any unsolved question lay upon his mind like a personal grievance until it was settled to his full understanding. One plant after another, with its sand-covered roots, went into his pockets, his handkerchief and the 'full' of his shirt, until he was bulbing and sprouting all over and could carry no more. He was taking them to the boat to analyse and compare at leisure. Then he began to requisition my receptacles. I stood it while he stuffed my pockets, but rebelled when he tried to poke the prickly, scratchy things inside my shirt. I had not yet attained that sublime indifference to physical comfort, that Nirvana of passivity, that Muir had found.

Hours had passed in this entrancing work and we were progressing upwards but slowly. We were on the southeastern slope of the mountain, and the sun was still staring at us from a cloudless sky. Suddenly we were in the shadow as we worked around a spur of rock. Muir looked up, startled. Then he jammed home his last handful of plants, and hastened up to where I stood.

'Man!' he said, 'I was forgetting. We'll have to hurry now or we'll miss it, we'll miss it.'

'Miss what?' I asked.

'The jewel of the day,' he answered; 'the sight of the sunset from the top.'

Then Muir began to *slide* up that mountain. I had been with mountain climbers before, but never one like him. A deer-lope over the smoother slopes, a sure instinct for the easiest way into a rocky fortress, an instant and unerring attack, a serpent-glide up the steep; eye, hand and foot all connected dynamically; with no appearance of weight to his body – as though he had Stockton's negative gravity machine strapped on his back.

Fifteen years of enthusiastic study among the Sierras had given him the same pre-eminence over the ordinary climber as the Big Horn of the Rockies shows over the Cotswold. It was only by exerting myself to the limit of my strength that I was able to keep near him. His example was at the same time my inspiration and despair. I longed for him to stop and rest, but would not have suggested it for the world. I would at least be game, and furnish no hint as to how tired I was, no matter how chokingly my heart thumped. Muir's spirit was in me, and my 'chief end', just then, was to win that peak with him. The impending calamity of being beaten by the sun was not to be contemplated without horror. The loss of a fortune would be as nothing to that!

We were now beyond the flower garden of the gods, in a land of rocks and cliffs, with patches of short grass, caribou moss and lichens between. Along a narrowing arm of the mountain, a deep canyon flumed a rushing torrent of icy water from a small glacier on our right. Then came moraine matter, rounded pebbles and boulders, and beyond them the glacier. Once a giant, it is nothing but a baby now, but the ice is still blue and clear, and the crevasses many and deep. And that day it had to be crossed, which was a ticklish task. A misstep or slip might land us at once fairly into the heart of the glacier, there to be preserved in cold storage for the wonderment of future generations. But glaciers were Muir's special pets, his intimate companions, with whom he held sweet communion. Their voices were plain language to his ears, their work, as God's landscape gardeners, of the wisest and best that Nature could offer.

No Swiss guide was ever wiser in the habits of glaciers than Muir, or proved to be a better pilot across their deathly crevasses. Half a mile of careful walking and jumping and we were on the ground again, at the base of the great cliff of metamorphic slate that crowned the summit. Muir's aneroid barometer showed a height of about 7000 feet, and the wall of rock towered threateningly above us, leaning out in places, 1000 feet or so above the glacier. But the earth-fires that had melted and heaved it, the ice mass that chiselled and shaped it, the wind and rain that corroded and crumbled it, had left plenty of bricks out of that battlement, had covered its face with knobs and horns, had ploughed ledges and cleaved fissures and fastened crags and pinnacles upon it, so that, while its surface was full of man-traps and blind ways, the human spider might still find some hold for his claws.

The shadows were dark upon us, but the lofty, icy peaks of the main range still lay bathed in the golden rays of the setting sun. There was no time to be lost. A quick glance to the right and left, and Muir, who had steered his course wisely across the glacier, attacked the cliff, simply saying, 'We must climb cautiously here.'

Now came the most wonderful display of his mountaincraft. Had I been alone at the feet of these crags I should have said, 'It can't be done', and have turned back down the mountain. But Muir was my 'control', as the Spiritists say, and I never thought of doing anything else but following him. He thought he could climb up there and that settled it. He would do what he thought he could. And such climbing! There was never an instant when both feet and hands were not in play, and often elbows, knees, thighs, upper arms, and even chin must grip and hold. Clambering up a steep slope, crawling under an overhanging rock, spreading out like a flying squirrel and edging along an inch-wide projection while fingers clasped knobs above the head, bending about sharp angles, pulling up smooth rock-faces by sheer strength of arm and chinning over the edge, leaping fissures, sliding flat around a dangerous rock-breast, testing crumbly spurs before risking his weight, always going up, up, no hesitation, no pause – that was Muir! My task was the lighter one; he did the head-work, I had but to imitate. The thin fragment of projecting slate that stood the weight of his 150 pounds would surely sustain my 130. As far as possible I did as he did, took his handholds, and stepped in his steps.

But I was handicapped in a way that Muir was ignorant of, and I would not tell him for fear of his veto upon my climbing. My legs were all right – hard and sinewy; my body light and supple, my wind good, my nerves steady (heights did not make me dizzy); but my arms – there lay the trouble. Ten years before I had been fond of breaking colts – till the colts broke me. On successive summers in West Virginia, two colts had fallen with me and dislocated first my left shoulder, then my right. Since that, both arms had been out of joint more than once. My left was especially weak. It would not sustain my weight, and I had to favour it constantly. Now and again, as I pulled myself up some difficult reach I could feel the head of the humerus move from its socket.

Muir climbed so fast that his movements were almost like flying, legs and arms moving with perfect precision and unfailing judgement. I must keep close behind him or I would fail to see his points of vantage. But the pace was a killing one for me. As we neared the summit my strength began to fail, my breath to come in gasps, my muscles to twitch. The overwhelming fear of losing sight of my guide, of being left behind and failing to see that sunset, grew upon me, and I hurled myself blindly at every fresh obstacle, determined to keep up. At length we climbed upon a little shelf, a foot or two wide, that corkscrewed to the left. Here we paused a moment to take breath and look around us. We had ascended the cliff some 950 feet from the glacier, and were within forty or fifty feet of the top.

Among the much-prized gifts of this good world one of the very richest was given to me in that hour. It is securely locked in the safe of my memory and nobody can rob me of it – an imperishable treasure. Standing out on the rounded neck of the cliff and facing the southwest, we could see on three sides of us. The view was much the finest of all my experience. We seemed to stand on a high rostrum in the centre of the greatest amphitheatre in the world. The sky was cloudless, the level sun flooding all the landscape with golden light. From the base of the mountain on which we stood stretched the rolling upland. Striking boldly across our front was the deep valley of the Stickeen, a line of foliage, light green cottonwoods and darker alders, sprinkled with black fir and spruce, through which the river gleamed with a silvery sheen, now spreading wide among its islands, now foaming white through narrow canyons. Beyond, among the undulating hills, was a marvellous array of lakes. There must have been thirty or forty of them, from the pond of an acre, to the wide sheet two or three miles across. The strangely elongated and rounded hills had the appearance of giants in bed, wrapped in many-coloured blankets, while the lakes were their deep, blue eyes, lashed with dark evergreens, gazing steadfastly heavenward. Look long at these recumbent forms and you will see the heaving of their breasts. The whole landscape was alert, expectant of glory. Around this great camp of prostrate Cyclops there stood an unbroken semicircle of mighty peaks in solemn grandeur, some hoary-headed, some with locks of brown, but all wearing white glacier collars. The taller peaks seemed almost sharp enough to be the helmets and spears of watchful sentinels. And the colours! Great stretches of crimson fireweed, acres and acres of them, smaller patches of dark blue lupins, and hills of shaded yellow, red, and brown, the many-shaded green of the woods, the amethyst and purple of the far horizon – who can tell it? We did not stand there more than two or three minutes, but the whole wonderful scene is deeply etched on the tablet of my memory, a photogravure never to be effaced.

Muir was the first to awake from his trance. Nothing could slake his wild thirst of desire. 'The sunset,' he cried; 'we must have the whole horizon.'

Then he started running along the ledge like a mountain goat, working to get around the vertical cliff above us to find an ascent on the other side. He was soon out of sight, although I followed as fast as I could. I heard him shout something, but could not make out his words. I know now he was warning me of a dangerous place. Then I came to a sharp-cut fissure which lay across my path – a gash in the rock, as if one of the Cyclops had struck it with his axe. It sloped very steeply for some twelve feet below, opening on the face of the precipice above the glacier, and was filled to within about four feet of the surface with flat, slaty gravel. It was only four or five feet across, and I could easily have leaped it had I not been so tired. But a rock the size of my head projected from the slippery stream of gravel. In my haste to overtake Muir I did not stop to make sure this stone was part of the cliff, but stepped with springing force upon it to cross the fissure. Instantly the stone melted away beneath my feet, and I shot with it down towards the precipice. With my peril sharp upon me I cried out as I whirled on my face, and struck out both hands to grasp the rock on either side.

Falling forward hard, my hands struck the walls of the chasm, my arms were twisted behind me, and instantly both shoulders were dislocated. With my paralysed arms flopping helplessly above my head, I slid swiftly down the narrow chasm. Instinctively I flattened down on the sliding gravel, digging my chin and toes into it to check my descent; but not until my feet hung out over the edge of the cliff did I feel that I had stopped. Even then I dared not breathe or stir, so precarious was my hold on that treacherous shale. Every moment I seemed to be slipping inch by inch to the point when all would give way and I would go whirling down to the glacier.

After the first wild moment of panic when I felt myself falling, I do not remember any sense of fear. But I know what it is to have a thousand thoughts flash through the brain in a single instant – an anguished thought of my young wife at Wrangell, with her imminent motherhood; an indignant thought of the insurance companies that refused me policies on my life; a thought of wonder as to what would become of my poor flocks of Indians among the islands; recollections of events far and near in time, important and trivial; but each thought printed upon my memory by the instantaneous photography of deadly peril. I had no hope of escape at all. The gravel was rattling past me and piling up against my head. The jar of a little rock, and all would be over. The situation was too desperate for actual fear. Dull wonder as to how long I would be in the air, and the hope that death would be instant – that was all. Then came the wish that Muir would come before I fell, and take a message to my wife.

Suddenly I heard his voice right above me. 'My God!' he cried. Then he added, 'Grab that rock, man, just by your right hand.'

I gurgled from my throat, not daring to inflate my lungs, 'My arms are out.'

There was a pause. Then his voice rang again, cheery, confident, unexcited, 'Hold fast; I'm going to get you out of this. I can't get to you on this side; the rock is sheer. I'll have to leave you now and cross the rift high up and come down to you on the other side by which we came. Keep cool.'

Then I heard him going away, whistling 'The Blue Bells of Scotland', singing snatches of Scotch songs, calling to me, his voice now receding, as the rocks intervened, then sounding louder as he came out on the face of the cliff. But in me hope surged at full tide. I entertained no more thoughts of last messages. I did not see how he could possibly do it, but he was John Muir, and I had seen his wonderful rock-work. So I determined not to fall and made myself as flat and heavy as possible, not daring to twitch a muscle or wink an eyelid, for I still felt myself slipping, slipping down the greasy slate. And now a new peril threatened. A chill ran through me of cold and nervousness, and I slid an inch. I suppressed the growing shivers with all my will. I would keep perfectly quiet till Muir came back. The sickening pain in my shoulders increased till it was torture, and I could not ease it.

It seemed like hours, but it was really only about ten minutes before he got back to me. By that time I hung so far over the edge of the precipice that it seemed impossible that I could last another second.

Now I heard Muir's voice, low and steady, close to me, and it seemed a little below. 'Hold steady,' he said. 'I'll have to swing you out over the cliff.'

Then I felt a careful hand on my back, fumbling with the waistband of my pants, my vest and shirt, gathering all in a firm grip. I could see only with one eye and that looked upon but a foot or two of gravel on the other side.

'Now!' he said, and I slid out of the cleft with a rattling shower of stones and gravel. My head swung down, my impotent arms dangling, and I stared straight at the glacier, 1000 feet below. Then my feet came against the cliff.

'Work downwards with your feet.'

I obeyed. He drew me close to him by crooking his arm and as my head came up past his level he caught me by my collar with his teeth! My feet struck the little two-inch shelf on which he was standing, and I could see Muir, flattened against the face of the rock and facing it, his right hand stretched up and clasping a little spur, his left holding me with an iron grip, his head bent sideways, as my weight drew it. I felt as alert and cool as he.

'I've got to let go of you,' he hissed through his clenched teeth. 'I need both hands here. Climb upward with your feet.'

How he did it, I know not. The miracle grows as I ponder it. The wall was almost perpendicular and smooth. My weight on his jaws dragged him outwards. And yet, holding me by his teeth as a panther her cub and clinging like a squirrel to a tree, he climbed with me straight up ten or twelve feet, with only the help of my iron-shod feet scrambling on the rock. It was utterly impossible, yet he did it!

When he landed me on the little shelf along which we had come, my nerve gave way and I trembled all over. I sank down exhausted, Muir only less tired, but supporting me.

The sun had set; the air was icy cold and we had no coats. We would soon chill through. Muir's task of rescue had only begun and no time was to be lost. In a minute he was up again, examining my shoulders. The right one had an upward dislocation, the ball of the humerus resting on the process of the scapula, the rim of the cup. I told him how, and he soon snapped the bone into its socket. But the left was a harder proposition. The luxation was downward and forward, and the strong, nervous reaction of the muscles had pulled the head of the bone deep into my armpit. There was no room to work on that narrow ledge. All that could be done was to make a rude sling with one of my suspenders and our handkerchiefs, so as to both support the elbow and keep the arm from swinging.

Then came the task to get down that terrible wall to the glacier, by the only practicable way down the mountain that Muir, after a careful search, could find. Again I am at loss to know how he accomplished it. For an unencumbered man to descend it in the deepening dusk was a most difficult task; but to get a tottery, nerve-shaken, pain-wracked cripple down was a feat of positive wonder. My right arm, though in place, was almost helpless. I could only move my forearm; the muscles of the upper part simply refusing to obey my will. Muir would let himself down to a lower shelf, brace himself and I would get my right hand against him, crawl my fingers over his shoulder until the arm hung in front of him, and falling against him, would be eased down to his standing ground. Sometimes he would pack me a short distance on his back. Again, taking me by the wrist, he would swing me down to a lower shelf, before descending himself. My right shoulder came out three times that night, and had to be reset.

It was dark when we reached the base; there was no moon and it was very cold. The glacier provided an operating table, and I lay on the ice for an hour while Muir, having slit the sleeve of my shirt to the collar, tugged and twisted at my left arm in a vain attempt to set it. But the ball was too deep in its false socket, and all his pulling only bruised and made it swell. So be had to do up the arm again, and tie it tight to my body. It must have been near midnight when we left the foot of the cliff and started down the mountain. We had ten hard miles to go, and no supper, for the hardtack had disappeared ere we were halfway up the mountain. Muir dared not take me across the glacier in the dark; I was too weak to jump the crevasses. So we skirted it and came, after a mile, to the head of a great slide of gravel, the fine moraine matter of the receding glacier. Muir sat down on the gravel; I sat against him with my feet on either side and my arm over his shoulder. Then he began to hitch and kick, and presently we were sliding at great speed in a cloud of dust. A full half-mile we flew, and were almost buried when we reached the bottom of the slide. It was the easiest part of our trip.

Now we found ourselves in the canyon, down which tumbled the glacial stream, and far beneath the ridge along which we had ascended. The sides of the canyon were sheer cliffs.

'We'll try it,' said Muir. 'Sometimes these canyons are passable.'

But the way grew rougher as we descended. The rapids became falls and we often had to retrace our steps to find a way around them. After we reached the timber-line, some four miles from the summit, the going was still harder, for we had a thicket of alders and willows to fight. Here Muir offered to make a fire and leave me while he went forward for assistance, but I refused. 'No,' I said, 'I'm going to make it to the boat.'

All that night this man of steel and lightning worked, never resting a minute, doing the work of three men, helping me along the slopes, easing me down the rocks, pulling me up cliffs, dashing water on me when I grew faint with the pain; and always cheery, full of talk and anecdote, cracking jokes with me, infusing me with his own indomitable spirit. He was eyes, hands, feet, and heart to me – my caretaker, in whom I trusted absolutely. My eyes brim with tears even now when I think of his utter self-abandon as he ministered to my infirmities.

About four o'clock in the morning we came to a fall that we could not compass, sheer a hundred feet or more. So we had to attack the steep walls of the canyon. After a hard struggle we were on the mountain ridges again, traversing the flower pastures, creeping through openings in the brush, scrambling over the dwarf fir, then down through the fallen timber. It was half-past seven o'clock when we descended the last slope and found the path to Glenora. Here we met a straggling party of whites and Indians just starting out to search the mountain for us.

As I was coming wearily up the teetering gangplank, feeling as if I couldn't keep up another minute, Dr Kendall stepped upon its end, barring my passage, bent his bushy white brows upon me from his six feet of height, and began to scold:

'See here, young man; give an account of yourself. Do you know you've kept us waiting –'

Just then Captain Lane jumped forward to help me, digging the old Doctor of Divinity with his elbow in the stomach and nearly knocking him off the boat.

'Oh, hell!' he roared. 'Can't you see the man's hurt?'

Mrs Kendall was a very tall, thin, severe-looking old lady, with face lined with grief by the loss of her children. She never smiled. She had not gone to bed at all that night, but walked the deck and would not let her husband or the others sleep. Soon after daylight she began to lash the men with the whip of her tongue for their 'cowardice and inhumanity' in not starting at once to search for me.

'Mr Young is undoubtedly lying mangled at the foot of a cliff, or else one of those terrible bears has wounded him; and you are lolling around here instead of starting to his rescue. For shame!'

When they objected that they did not know where we had gone, she snapped: 'Go everywhere until you find him.'

Her fierce energy started the men we met. When I came on board she at once took charge and issued her orders, which everybody jumped to obey. She had blankets spread on the floor of the cabin and laid me on them. She obtained some whisky from the captain, some water, porridge and coffee from the steward. She was sitting on the floor with my head in her lap, feeding me coffee with a spoon, when Dr Kendall came in and began on me again:

'Suppose you had fallen down that precipice, what would your poor wife have done? What would have become of your Indians and your new church?'

Then Mrs Kendall turned and thrust her spoon like a sword at him. 'Henry Kendall,' she blazed, 'shut right up and leave this room. Have you no sense? Go instantly, I say!' And the good Doctor went.

My recollections of that day are not very clear. The shoulder was in a bad condition – swollen, bruised, very painful. I had to be strengthened with food and rest, and Muir called from his sleep of exhaustion, so that with four other men he could pull and twist that poor arm of mine for an hour. They got it into its socket, but scarcely had Muir got to sleep again before the strong, nervous twitching of the shoulder dislocated it a second time and seemingly placed it in a worse condition than before. Captain Lane was now summoned, and with Muir to direct, they worked for two or three hours. Whisky was poured down my throat to relax my stubborn, pain-convulsed muscles. Then they went at it with two men pulling at the towel knotted about my wrist, two others pulling against them, foot braced to foot, Muir manipulating my shoulder with his sinewy hands, and the stocky Captain, strong and compact as a bear, with his heel against the yarn ball in my armpit, takes me by the elbow and says, 'I'll set it or pull the arm off!'

Well, he almost does the latter. I am conscious of a frightful strain, a spasm of anguish in my side as his heel slips from the ball and kicks in two of my ribs, a snap as the head of the bone slips into the cup – then kindly oblivion.

I was awakened about five o'clock in the afternoon by the return of the whole party from an excursion to the Great Glacier at the Boundary Line. Muir, fresh and enthusiastic as ever, had been the pilot across the moraine and upon the great ice mountain; and I, wrapped like a mummy in linen strips, was able to join in his laughter as he told of the big D.D.'s heroics, when, in the middle of an acre of alder brush, he asked indignantly, in response to the hurry-up calls: 'Do you think I'm going to leave my wife in this forest?'

One overpowering regret – one only – abides in my heart as I think back upon that golden day with John Muir. He could, and did, go back to Glenora on the return trip of the *Cassiar*, ascend the mountain again, see the sunset from its top, make charming sketches, stay all night and see the sunrise, filling his cup of joy so full that he could pour out entrancing descriptions for days. While I – well, with entreating arms about one's neck and pleading, tearful eyes looking into one's own, what could one do but promise to climb no more? But my lifelong lamentation over a treasure forever lost, is this: 'I never saw the sunset from that peak.'

THE STICKEEN RIVER

John Muir

John Muir's own account of his first 1879 trip to Alaska and of his
rescue of Samuel Hall Young on Glenora Peak, published in 1915 after
Muir's death as part of *Travels in Alaska.*[1]

The most interesting of the short excursions we made from Fort
Wrangell was the one up the Stickeen River to the head of steam
navigation. From Mount St Elias the Coast Range extends in a broad,
lofty chain beyond the southern boundary of the territory, gashed by
stupendous canyons, each of which carries a lively river, though most
of them are comparatively short, as their highest sources lie in the icy
solitudes of the range within forty or fifty miles of the coast. A few,
however, of these foaming, roaring streams – the Alsek, Chilcat,
Chilcoot, Taku, Stickeen, and perhaps others – head beyond the
range with some of the southwest branches of the Mackenzie and
Yukon.

The largest side branches of the maintrunk canyons of all these
mountain streams are still occupied by glaciers which descend in
showy ranks, their massy, bulging snouts lying back a little distance in
the shadows of the walls, or pushing forward among the cotton-
woods that line the banks of the rivers, or even stretching all the way
across the main canyons, compelling the rivers to find a channel
beneath them.

The Stickeen was, perhaps, the best known of the rivers that cross
the Coast Range, because it was the best way to the Mackenzie River
Cassiar gold-mines. It is about 350 miles long, and is navigable for
small steamers 150 miles to Glenora, and sometimes to Telegraph
Creek, fifteen miles farther. It first pursues a westerly course through
grassy plains darkened here and there with groves of spruce and pine;

then, curving southward and receiving numerous tributaries from the north, it enters the Coast Range, and sweeps across it through a magnificent canyon three thousand to five thousand feet deep, and more than a hundred miles long. The majestic cliffs and mountains forming the canyon walls display endless variety of form and sculpture, and are wonderfully adorned and enlivened with glaciers and waterfalls, while throughout almost its whole extent the floor is a flowery landscape garden, like Yosemite. The most striking features are the glaciers, hanging over the cliffs, descending the side canyons and pushing forward to the river, greatly enhancing the wild beauty of all the others.

Gliding along the swift-flowing river, the views change with bewildering rapidity. Wonderful, too, are the changes dependent on the seasons and the weather. In spring, when the snow is melting fast, you enjoy the countless rejoicing waterfalls; the gentle breathing of warm winds; the colours of the young leaves and flowers when the bees are busy and wafts of fragrance are drifting hither and thither from miles of wild roses, clover, and honeysuckle; the swaths of birch and willow on the lower slopes following the melting of the winter avalanche snow-banks; the bossy cumuli swelling in white and purple piles above the highest peaks; grey rain-clouds wreathing the out-standing brows and battlements of the walls; and the breaking-forth of the sun after the rain; the shining of the leaves and streams and crystal architecture of the glaciers; the rising of fresh fragrance; the song of the happy birds; and the serene colour-grandeur of the morning and evening sky. In summer you find the groves and gardens in full dress; glaciers melting rapidly under sunshine and rain; waterfalls in all their glory; the river rejoicing in its strength; young birds trying their wings; bears enjoying salmon and berries; all the life of the canyon brimming full like the streams. In autumn comes rest, as if the year's work were done. The rich, hazy sunshine streaming over the cliffs calls forth the last of the gentians and goldenrods; the groves and thickets and meadows bloom again as their leaves change to red and yellow petals; the rocks also, and the glaciers, seem to bloom like the plants in the mellow golden light. And so goes the song, change succeeding change in sublime harmony through all the wonderful seasons and weather.

My first trip up the river was made in the spring with the missionary party soon after our arrival at Wrangell. We left Wrangell in the afternoon and anchored for the night above the river delta, and started up the river early next morning when the heights above the "Big Stickeen" Glacier and the smooth domes and copings and arches of solid snow along the tops of the canyon walls were glowing in the early beams. We arrived before noon at the old trading-post called "Buck's" in front of the Stickeen Glacier, and remained long enough to allow the few passengers who wished a nearer view to cross the river to the terminal moraine. The sunbeams streaming through the ice pinnacles along its terminal wall produced a wonderful glory of colour, and the broad, sparkling crystal prairie and the distant snowy fountains were wonderfully attractive and made me pray for opportunity to explore them.

Of the many glaciers, a hundred or more, that adorn the walls of the great Stickeen River Canyon, this is the largest. It draws its sources from snowy mountains within fifteen or twenty miles of the coast, pours through a comparatively narrow canyon about two miles in width in a magnificent cascade, and expands in a broad fan five or six miles in width, separated from the Stickeen River by its broad terminal moraine, fringed with spruces and willows. Around the beautifully drawn curve of the moraine the Stickeen River flows, having evidently been shoved by the glacier out of its direct course. On the opposite side of the canyon another somewhat smaller glacier, which now terminates four or five miles from the river, was once united front to front with the greater glacier, though at first both were tributaries of the main Stickeen Glacier which once filled the whole grand canyon. After the main trunk canyon was melted out, its side branches, drawing their sources from a height of three or four to five or six thousand feet, were cut off, and of course became separate glaciers, occupying cirques and branch canyons along the tops and sides of the walls. The Indians have a tradition that the river used to run through a tunnel under the united fronts of the two large tributary glaciers mentioned above, which entered the main canyon from either side; and that on one occasion an Indian, anxious to get rid of his wife, had her sent adrift in a canoe down through the ice tunnel, expecting that she would trouble him no more. But to his surprise she floated through under the ice in safety. All the evidence connected with the present appearance of these two glaciers indicates that they were united and formed a dam across the river after the smaller tributaries had been melted off and had receded to a greater or lesser height above the valley floor.

The Big Stickeen Glacier is hardly out of sight ere you come upon another that pours a majestic crystal flood through the evergreens, while almost every hollow and tributary canyon contains a smaller one, the size, of course, varying with the extent of the area drained. Some are like mere snow-banks; others, with the blue ice apparent, depend in massive bulging curves and swells, and graduate into the river-like forms that maze through the lower forested regions and are so striking and beautiful that they are admired even by the passing miners with gold-dust in their eyes.

Thirty-five miles above the Big Stickeen Glacier is the 'Dirt Glacier', the second in size. Its outlet is a fine stream, abounding in trout. On the opposite side of the river there is a group of five glaciers, one of them descending to within a hundred feet of the river.

Near Glenora, on the northeastern flank of the main Coast Range, just below a narrow gorge called 'The Canyon', terraces first make their appearance, where great quantities of moraine material have been swept through the flood-choked gorge and of course outspread and deposited on the first open levels below. Here, too, occurs a marked change in climate and consequently in forests and general appearance of the face of the country. On account of destructive fires the woods are younger and are composed of smaller trees about a foot to eighteen inches in diameter and seventy-five feet high, mostly two-leafed pines which hold their seeds for several years after they are ripe. The woods here are without a trace of those deep accumulations of mosses, leaves, and decaying trunks which make so damp and unclearable a mass in the coast forests. Whole mountainsides are covered with grey moss and lichens where the forest has been utterly destroyed. The riverbank cotton-woods are also smaller, and the birch and contorta pines mingle freely with the coast hemlock and spruce. The birch is common on the lower slopes and is very effective, its round, leafy, pale green head contrasting with the dark, narrow spires of the conifers and giving a striking character to the forest. The 'tamarack pine' or black pine, as the variety of *P. contorta* is called here, is yellowish-green, in marked contrast with the dark, lichen-draped spruce which grows above the pine at a height of about 2000 feet, in groves and belts where it has escaped fire and snow avalanches. There is another handsome spruce hereabouts, *Picea alba*, very slender and graceful in habit, drooping at the top like a mountain hemlock. I saw fine specimens 125 feet high on deep bottom land a few miles below Glenora. The tops of some of them were almost covered with dense clusters of yellow and brown cones.

We reached the old Hudson's Bay trading-post at Glenora about one o'clock, and the captain informed me that he would stop here until the next morning, when he would make an early start for Wrangell.

At a distance of about seven or eight miles to the northeastward of the landing, there is an outstanding group of mountains crowning a spur from the main chain of the Coast Range, whose highest point rises about 8000 feet above the level of the sea; and as Glenora is only a thousand feet above the sea, the height to be overcome in climbing this peak is about 7000 feet. Though the time was short I determined to climb it, because of the advantageous position it occupied for general views of the peaks and glaciers of the east side of the great range.

Although it was now twenty minutes past three and the days were getting short, I thought that by rapid climbing I could reach the summit before sunset, in time to get a general view and a few pencil sketches, and make my way back to the steamer in the night. Mr Young, one of the missionaries, asked permission to accompany me, saying that he was a good walker and climber and would not delay me or cause any trouble. I strongly advised him not to go, explaining that it involved a walk, coming and going, of fourteen or sixteen miles, and a climb through brush and boulders of 7000 feet, a fair day's work for a seasoned mountaineer to be done in less than half a day and part of a night. But he insisted that he was a strong walker, could do a mountaineer's day's work in half a day, and would not hinder me in any way.

'Well, I have warned you,' I said, 'and will not assume responsibility for any trouble that may arise.'

He proved to be a stout walker, and we made rapid progress across a brushy timbered flat and up the mountain slopes, open in some places, and in others thatched with dwarf firs, resting a minute here and there to refresh ourselves with huckleberries, which grew in abundance in open spots. About half an hour before sunset, when we were near a cluster of crumbling pinnacles that formed the summit, I had ceased to feel anxiety about the mountaineering strength and skill of my companion, and pushed rapidly on. In passing around the shoulder of the highest pinnacle, where the rock was rapidly disintegrating and the danger of slipping was great, I shouted in a warning voice, 'Be very careful here, this is dangerous.'

Mr Young was perhaps a dozen or two yards behind me, but out of sight. I afterwards reproached myself for not stopping and lending him a steadying hand, and showing him the slight footsteps I had made by kicking out little blocks of the crumbling surface, instead of simply warning him to be careful. Only a few seconds after giving this warning, I was startled by a scream for help, and hurrying back, found the missionary face downward, his arms outstretched, clutching little crumbling knobs on the brink of a gully that plunges down 1000 feet or more to a small residual glacier. I managed to get below him, touched one of his feet, and tried to encourage him by saying, 'I am below you. You are in no danger. You can't slip past me and I will soon get you out of this.'

He then told me that both of his arms were dislocated. It was almost impossible to find available footholds on the treacherous rock, and I was at my wits' end to know how to get him rolled or dragged to a place where I could get about him, find out how much he was hurt, and a way back down the mountain. After narrowly scanning the cliff and making footholds, I managed to roll and lift him a few yards to a place where the slope was less steep, and there I attempted to set his arms. I found, however, that this was impossible in such a place. I therefore tied his arms to his sides with my suspenders and necktie, to prevent as much as possible inflammation from movement. I then left him, telling him to lie still, that I would be back in a few minutes, and that he was now safe from slipping. I hastily examined the ground and saw no way of getting him down except by the steep glacier gully. After scrambling to an outstanding point that commands a view of it from top to bottom, to make sure that it was not interrupted by sheer precipices, I concluded that with great care and the digging of slight footholds he could be slid down to the glacier, where I could lay him on his back and perhaps be able to set his arms. Accordingly, I cheered him up, telling him I had found a way, but that it would require lots of time and patience. Digging a footstep in the sand or crumbling rock five or six feet beneath him, I reached up, took hold of him by one of his feet, and gently slid him down on his back, placed his heels in the step, then descended another five or six feet, dug heel notches, and slid him down to them. Thus the whole distance was made by a succession of narrow steps at very short intervals, and the glacier was reached perhaps about midnight. Here I took off one of my boots, tied a handkerchief around his wrist for a good hold, placed my heel in his arm pit, and succeeded in getting one of his arms into place, but my utmost strength was insufficient to reduce the dislocation of the other. I therefore bound it closely to his side, and asked him if in his exhausted and trembling condition he was still able to walk.

'Yes,' he bravely replied.

So, with a steadying arm around him and many stops for rest, I marched him slowly down in the starlight on the comparatively smooth, unfissured surface of the little glacier to the terminal moraine, a distance of perhaps a mile, crossed the moraine, bathed his head at one of the outlet streams, and after many rests reached a dry place and made a brush fire. I then went ahead looking for an open way through the bushes to where larger wood could be had, made a good lasting fire of resiny silver-fir roots, and a leafy bed beside it. I now told him I would run down the mountain, hasten back with help from the boat, and carry him down in comfort. But he would not hear of my leaving him.

'No, no,' he said, 'I can walk down. Don't leave me.'

I reminded him of the roughness of the way, his nerve-shaken condition, and assured him I would not be gone long. But he insisted on trying, saying on no account whatever must I leave him. I therefore concluded to try to get him to the ship by short walks from one fire and resting-place to another. While he was resting I went ahead, looking for the best way through the brush and rocks, then returning, got him on his feet and made him lean on my shoulder while I steadied him to prevent his falling. This slow, staggering struggle from fire to fire lasted until long after sunrise. When at last we reached the ship and stood at the foot of the narrow single plank without side rails that reached from the bank to the deck at a considerable angle, I briefly explained to Mr Young's companions, who stood looking down at us, that he had been hurt in an accident, and requested one of them to assist me in getting him aboard. But strange to say, instead of coming down to help, they made haste to reproach him for having gone on a 'wild-goose chase' with Muir.

'These foolish adventures are well enough for Mr Muir,' they said, 'but you, Mr Young, have a work to do; you have a family; you have a church, and you have no right to risk your life on treacherous peaks and precipices.'

The captain, Nat Lane, son of Senator Joseph Lane, had been swearing in angry impatience for being compelled to make so late a start and thus encounter a dangerous wind in a narrow gorge, and was threatening to put the missionaries ashore to seek their lost companion, while he went on down the river about his business. But when he heard my call for help, he hastened forward, and elbowed the divines away from the end of the gangplank, shouting in angry irreverence, 'Oh, blank! This is no time for preaching! Don't you see the man is hurt?'

He ran down to our help, and while I steadied my trembling companion from behind, the captain kindly led him up the plank into the saloon, and made him drink a large glass of brandy. Then, with a man holding down his shoulders, we succeeded in getting the bone into its socket, notwithstanding the inflammation and contraction of the muscles and ligaments. Mr Young was then put to bed, and he slept all the way back to Wrangell.

In his mission lectures in the East, Mr Young oftentimes told this story. I made no record of it in my notebook and never intended to write a word about it; but after a miserable, sensational caricature of the story had appeared in a respectable magazine, I thought it but fair to my brave companion that it should be told just as it happened.

NOTES:
1. The Stickeen River is located in present-day British Columbia and is spelled 'Stikine'.

12

GLENORA PEAK

John Muir

This is John Muir's account of his second ascent of Glenora in 1880, which he made the year after his rescue of Samuel Hall Young. It was published after Muir's death as part of *Travels in Alaska* in 1915.

On the trail to the steamboat – landing at the foot of Dease Lake, I met a Douglas squirrel, nearly as red and rusty in colour as his Eastern relative the chickaree. Except in colour he differs but little from the California Douglas squirrel. In voice, language, gestures, temperament he is the same fiery indomitable little king of the woods. Another darker and probably younger specimen met near the Caribou House, barked, chirruped, and showed off in fine style on a tree within a few feet of us.

'What does the little rascal mean?' said my companion, a man I had fallen in with on the trail. 'What is he making such a fuss about? I cannot frighten him.'

'Never mind,' I replied; 'just wait until I whistle "Old Hundred" and you will see him fly in disgust.' And so he did, just as his California brethren do. Strange that no squirrel or spermophile I yet have found ever seemed to have anything like enough of Scotch religion to enjoy this grand old tune.

The taverns along the Cassiar gold trail were the worst I had ever seen, rough shacks with dirt floors, dirt roofs, and rough meals. The meals are all alike – a potato, a slice of something like bacon, some grey stuff called bread, and a cup of muddy, semi-liquid coffee like that which the California miners call 'slickens' or 'slumgullion'. The bread was terrible and sinful. How the Lord's good wheat could be made into stuff so mysteriously bad is past finding out. The very de'il, it would seem, in wicked anger and ingenuity, had been the baker.

On our walk from Dease Lake to Telegraph Creek we had one of these rough luncheons at three o'clock in the afternoon of the first day, then walked on five miles to Ward's, where we were solemnly assured that we could not have a single bite of either supper or breakfast, but as a great favour we might sleep on his best grey bunk. We replied that, as we had lunched at the lake, supper would not be greatly missed, and as for breakfast we would start early and walk eight miles to the next road-house. We set out at half-past four, glad to escape into the fresh air, and reached the breakfast place at eight o'clock. The landlord was still abed, and when at length he came to the door, he scowled savagely at us as if our request for breakfast was preposterous and criminal beyond anything ever heard of in all goldful Alaska. A good many in those days were returning from the mines dead broke, and he probably regarded us as belonging to that disreputable class. Anyhow, we got nothing and had to tramp on.

As we approached the next house, three miles ahead, we saw the tavern-keeper keenly surveying us, and, as we afterwards learned, taking me for a certain judge whom for some cause he wished to avoid, he hurriedly locked his door and fled. Half a mile farther on we discovered him in a thicket a little way off the trail, explained our wants, marched him back to his house, and at length obtained a little sour bread, sour milk, and old salmon, our only lonely meal between the Lake and Telegraph Creek.

We arrived at Telegraph Creek, the end of my 200-mile walk, about noon. After luncheon I went on down the river to Glenora in a fine canoe owned and manned by Kitty, a stout, intelligent looking Indian woman, who charged her passengers a dollar for the fifteen-mile trip. Her crew was four Indian paddlers. In the rapids she also plied the paddle, with stout, telling strokes, and a keen-eyed old man, probably her husband, sat high in the stern and steered. All seemed exhilarated as we shot down through the narrow gorge on the rushing, roaring, throttled river, paddling all the more vigorously the faster the speed of the stream, to hold good steering way. The canoe danced lightly amid grey surges and spray as if alive and enthusiastically enjoying the adventure. Some of the passengers were pretty thoroughly drenched. In unskilful hands the frail dugout would surely have been wrecked or upset. Most of the season, goods for the Cassiar gold camps were carried from Glenora to Telegraph Creek in canoes, the steamers not being able to overcome the rapids except during high water. Even then they had usually to line two of the rapids – that is, take a line ashore, make it fast to a tree on the bank, and pull up on the capstan. The freight canoes carried about three or four tons, for which fifteen dollars per ton was charged. Slow progress was made by poling along the bank out of the swiftest part of the current. In the rapids a towline was taken ashore, only one of the crew remaining aboard to steer. The trip took a day unless a favouring wind was blowing, which often happened.

Next morning I set out from Glenora to climb Glenora Peak for the general view of the great Coast Range that I failed to obtain on my first ascent on account of the accident that befell Mr Young when we were within a minute or two of the top. It is hard to fail in reaching a mountain-top that one starts for, let the cause be what it may. This time I had no companion to care for, but the sky was threatening. I was assured by the local weather-prophets that the day would be rainy or snowy because the peaks in sight were muffled in clouds that seemed to be getting ready for work. I determined to go ahead, however, for storms of any kind are well worthwhile, and if driven back I could wait and try again.

With crackers in my pocket and a light rubber coat that a kind Hebrew passenger on the steamer *Gertrude* loaned me, I was ready for anything that might offer, my hopes for the grand view rising and falling as the clouds rose and fell. Anxiously I watched them as they trailed their draggled skirts across the glaciers and fountain peaks as if thoughtfully looking for the places where they could do the most good. From Glenora there is first a terrace 200 feet above the river covered mostly with bushes, yellow apocynum on the open spaces, together with carpets of dwarf manzanita, bunch-grass, and a few of the compositæ, galliums, etc. Then comes a flat stretch a mile wide, extending to the foothills, covered with birch, spruce, fir, and poplar, now mostly killed by fire and the ground strewn with charred trunks. From this black forest the mountain rises in rather steep slopes covered with a luxuriant growth of bushes, grass, flowers, and a few trees, chiefly spruce and fir, the firs gradually dwarfing into a beautiful chaparral, the most beautiful, I think, I have ever seen, the flat fan-shaped plumes thickly foliaged and imbricated by snow pressure, forming a smooth, handsome thatch which bears cones and thrives as if this repressed condition were its very best. It extends up to an elevation of about 5500 feet. Only a few trees more than a foot in diameter and more than fifty feet high are found higher than 4000 feet above the sea. A few poplars and willows occur on moist places, gradually dwarfing like the conifers. Alder is the most generally distributed of the chaparral bushes, growing nearly everywhere; its crinkled stems an inch or two thick form a troublesome tangle to the mountaineer. The blue geranium, with leaves red and showy at this time of the year, is perhaps the most telling of the flowering plants. It grows up to 5000 feet or more. Larkspurs are common, with epilobium, senecio, erigeron, and a few solidagos.

The harebell appears at about 4000 feet and extends to the summit, dwarfing in stature but maintaining the size of its handsome bells until they seem to be lying loose and detached on the ground as if like snow flowers they had fallen from the sky; and, though frail and delicate-looking, none of its companions is more enduring or rings out the praise of beauty-loving Nature in tones more appreciable to mortals, not forgetting even Cassiope, who also is here and her companion, Bryanthus, the loveliest and most widely distributed of the alpine shrubs. Then come crowberry, and two species of huckleberry, one of them from about six inches to a foot high with delicious berries, the other a most lavishly prolific and contented looking dwarf, few of the bushes being more than two inches high, counting to the topmost leaf, yet each bearing from ten to twenty or more large berries. Perhaps more than half the bulk of the whole plant is fruit, the largest and finest-flavoured of all the huckleberries or blueberries I ever tasted, spreading fine feasts for the grouse and ptarmigan and many others of Nature's mountain people. I noticed three species of dwarf willows, one with narrow leaves, growing at the very summit of the mountain in cracks of the rocks, as well as on patches of soil, another with large, smooth leaves now turning yellow. The third species grows between the others as to elevation; its leaves, then orange coloured, are strikingly pitted and reticulated. Another alpine shrub, a species of sericocarpus, covered with handsome heads of feathery achenia, beautiful dwarf echiverias with flocks of purple flowers pricked into their bright grass-green, cushion-like bosses of moss-like foliage, and a fine forget-me-not reach to the summit. I may also mention a large mertensia, a fine anemone, a veratrum, six feet high, a large blue daisy, growing up to three to four thousand feet, and at the summit a dwarf species, with dusky, hairy involucres, and a few ferns, aspidium, gymnogramma, and small rock cheilanthes, leaving scarce a foot of ground bare, though the mountain looks bald and brown in the distance like those of the desert ranges of the Great Basin in Utah and Nevada.

Charmed with these plant people, I had almost forgotten to watch the sky until I reached the top of the highest peak, when one of the greatest and most impressively sublime of all the mountain views I have ever enjoyed came full in sight – more than 300 miles of closely packed peaks of the great Coast Range, sculptured in the boldest manner imaginable, their naked tops and dividing ridges dark in colour, their sides and the canyons, gorges, and valleys between them loaded with glaciers and snow. From this standpoint I counted upwards of two hundred glaciers, while dark-centred, luminous clouds with fringed edges hovered and crawled over them, now slowly descending, casting transparent shadows on the ice and snow, now rising high above them, lingering like loving angels guarding the crystal gifts they had bestowed. Although the range as seen from this Glenora mountain-top seems regular in its trend, as if the main axis were simple and continuous, it is, on the contrary, far from simple. In front of the highest ranks of peaks are others of the same form with their own glaciers, and lower peaks before these, and yet lower ones with their ridges and canyons, valleys and foothills. Alps rise beyond alps as far as the eye can reach, and clusters of higher peaks here and there closely crowded together; clusters, too, of needles and pinnacles innumerable like trees in groves. Everywhere the peaks seem comparatively slender and closely packed, as if Nature had here been trying to see how many noble well-dressed mountains could be crowded into one grand range.

The black rocks, too steep for snow to lie upon, were brought into sharp relief by white clouds and snow and glaciers, and these again were outlined and made tellingly plain by the rocks. The glaciers so grandly displayed are of every form, some crawling through gorge and valley like monster glittering serpents; others like broad cataracts pouring over cliffs into shadowy gulfs; others, with their main trunks winding through narrow canyons, display long, white finger-like tributaries descending from the summits of pinnacled ridges. Others lie back in fountain cirques walled in all around save at the lower edge, over which they pour in blue cascades. Snow, too, lay in folds and patches of every form on blunt, rounded ridges in curves, arrowy lines, dashes, and narrow ornamental flutings among the summit peaks and in broad, radiating wings on smooth slopes. And on many a bulging headland and lower ridge there lay heavy, over-curling copings and smooth, white domes where wind-driven snow was pressed and wreathed and packed into every form and in every possible place and condition. I never before had seen so richly sculptured a range or so many awe-inspiring inaccessible mountains crowded together. If a line were drawn east and west from the peak on which I stood, and extended both ways to the horizon, cutting the whole round landscape in two equal parts, then all of the south half would be bounded by these icy peaks, which would seem to curve around half the horizon and about twenty degrees more, though extending in a general straight, or but moderately curved, line. The deepest and thickest and highest of all this wilderness of peaks lie to the southwest. They are probably from about nine to twelve thousand feet high, springing to this elevation from near the sea level. The peak on which these observations were made is somewhere about 7000 feet high, and from here I estimated the height of the range. The highest peak of all, or that seemed so to me, lies to the westward at an estimated distance of about 150 or 200 miles. Only its solid white summit was visible. Possibly it may be the topmost peak of St Elias. Now look northward around the other half of the horizon, and instead of countless peaks crowding into the sky, you see a low, brown region, heaving and swelling in gentle curves, apparently scarcely more waved than a rolling prairie. The so-called canyons of several forks of the upper Stickeen are visible, but even where best seen in the foreground and middle ground of the picture, they are like mere sunken gorges, making scarce perceptible marks on the land-scape, while the tops of the highest mountain-swells show only small patches of snow and no glaciers.

Glenora Peak

Glenora Peak, on which I stood, is the highest point of a spur that puts out from the main range in a northerly direction. It seems to have been a rounded, broad-backed ridge, which has been sculptured into its present irregular form by short residual glaciers, some of which, a mile or two long, are still at work.

As I lingered, gazing on the vast show, luminous, shadowy clouds seemed to increase in glory of colour and motion, now fondling the highest peaks with infinite tenderness of touch, now hovering above them like eagles over their nests.

When night was drawing near, I ran down the flowery slopes exhilarated, thanking God for the gift of this great day. The setting sun fired the clouds. All the world seemed new-born. Every thing, even the commonest, was seen in new light and was looked at with new interest as if never seen before. The plant people seemed glad, as if rejoicing with me, the little ones as well as the trees, while every feature of the peak and its travelled boulders seemed to know what I had been about and the depth of my joy, as if they could read faces.

13

AN ASCENT OF MOUNT RAINIER

John Muir

Muir's own account of the ascent of Rainier of 14th August 1888, the
seventh recorded ascent, was published posthumously by his literary
executor in *Steep Trails* – 1918.

Ambitious climbers, seeking adventures and opportunities to test
their strength and skill, occasionally attempt to penetrate the
wilderness on the west side of the Sound, and push on to the
summit of Mount Olympus. But the grandest excursion of all to be
made hereabouts is to Mount Rainier, to climb to the top of its icy
crown. The mountain is very high, 14,400 feet, and laden with
glaciers that are terribly roughened and interrupted by crevasses
and ice-cliffs. Only good climbers should attempt to gain the
summit, led by a guide of proved nerve and endurance. A good
trail has been cut through the woods to the base of the mountain
on the north; but the summit of the mountain never has been
reached from this side, though many brave attempts have been
made upon it.

Last summer I gained the summit from the south side, in a day
and a half from the timber line, without encountering any desperate
obstacles that could not in some way be passed in good weather. I was
accompanied by Keith, the artist, Professor Ingraham, and five
ambitious young climbers from Seattle. We were led by the veteran
mountaineer and guide Van Trump, of Yelm, who many years before
guided General Stevens in his memorable ascent, and later Mr Bailey,
of Oakland. With a cumbersome abundance of campstools and
blankets we set out from Seattle, travelling by rail as far as Yelm
Prairie, on the Tacoma and Oregon road. Here we made our first
camp and arranged with Mr Longmire, a farmer in the neighbour-

hood, for pack and saddle animals. The noble King Mountain was in full view from here, glorifying the bright, sunny day with his presence, rising in godlike majesty over the woods, with the magnificent prairie as a foreground. The distance to the mountain from Yelm in a straight line is perhaps fifty miles; but by the mule and yellow-jacket trail we had to follow, it is a hundred miles. For, notwithstanding a portion of this trail runs in the air, where the wasps work hardest, it is far from being an air-line as commonly understood.

By night of the third day we reached the Soda Springs on the right bank of the Nisqually, which goes roaring by, grey with mud, gravel, and boulders from the caves of the glaciers of Rainier, now close at hand. The distance from the Soda Springs to the Camp of the Clouds is about ten miles. The first part of the way lies up the Nisqually Canyon, the bottom of which is flat in some places and the walls very high and precipitous, like those of the Yosemite Valley. The upper part of the canyon is still occupied by one of the Nisqually glaciers, from which this branch of the river draws its source, issuing from a cave in the grey, rock-strewn snout. About a mile below the glacier we had to ford the river, which caused some anxiety, for the current is very rapid and carried forward large boulders as well as lighter material, while its savage roar is bewildering.

At this point we left the canyon, climbing out of it by a steep zigzag up the old lateral moraine of the glacier, which was deposited when the present glacier flowed past at this height, and is about 800 feet high. It is now covered with a superb growth of *Picea amabilis*; so also is the corresponding portion of the right lateral. From the top of the moraine, still ascending, we passed for a mile or two through a forest of mixed growth, mainly silver fir, Patton spruce, and mountain pine, and then came to the charming park region, at an elevation of about 5000 feet above sea-level. Here the vast continuous woods at length begin to give way under the dominion of climate, though still at this height retaining their beauty and giving no sign of stress of storm, sweeping upward in belts of varying width, composed mainly of one species of fir, sharp and spiry in form, leaving smooth, spacious parks, with here and there separate groups of trees standing out in the midst of the openings like islands in a lake. Every one of these parks, great and small, is a garden filled knee-deep with fresh, lovely flowers of every hue, the most luxuriant and the most extravagantly beautiful of all the alpine gardens I ever beheld in all my mountain-top wanderings.

We arrived at the Cloud Camp at noon, but no clouds were in sight, save a few gauzy ornamental wreaths adrift in the sunshine. Out of the forest at last there stood the mountain, wholly unveiled, awful in bulk and majesty, filling all the view like a separate, new-born world, yet withal so fine and so beautiful it might well fire the dullest observer to desperate enthusiasm. Long we gazed in silent admiration, buried in tall daisies and anemones by the side of a snowbank. Higher we could not go with the animals and find food for them and wood for our own camp-fires, for just beyond this lies the region of ice, with only here and there an open spot on the ridges in the midst of the ice, with dwarf alpine plants, such as saxifrages and drabas, which reach far up between the glaciers, and low mats of the beautiful bryanthus, while back of us were the gardens and abundance of everything that heart could wish. Here we lay all the afternoon, considering the lilies and the lines of the mountains with reference to a way to the summit.

At noon next day we left camp and began our long climb. We were in light marching order, save one who pluckily determined to carry his camera to the summit. At night, after a long easy climb over wide and smooth fields of ice, we reached a narrow ridge, at an elevation of about 10,000 feet above the sea, on the divide between the glaciers of the Nisqually and the Cowlitz. Here we lay as best we could, waiting for another day, without fire of course, as we were now many miles beyond the timber line and without much to cover us. After eating a little hardtack, each of us levelled a spot to lie on among lava-blocks and cinders. The night was cold, and the wind coming down upon us in stormy surges drove gritty ashes and fragments of pumice about our ears while chilling to the bone. Very short and shallow was our sleep that night; but day dawned at last, early rising was easy, and there was nothing about breakfast to cause any delay. About four o'clock we were off, and climbing began in earnest. We followed up the ridge on which we had spent the night, now along its crest, now on either side, or on the ice leaning against it, until we came to where it becomes massive and precipitous. Then we were compelled to crawl along a seam or narrow shelf, on its face, which we traced to its termination in the base of the great ice-cap. From this point all the climbing was over ice, which was here desperately steep but fortunately was at the same time carved into innumerable spikes and pillars which afforded good footholds, and we crawled cautiously on, warm with ambition and exercise.

At length, after gaining the upper extreme of our guiding ridge, we found a good place to rest and prepare ourselves to scale the dangerous upper curves of the dome. The surface almost everywhere was bare, hard, snowless ice, extremely slippery; and, though smooth in general, it was interrupted by a network of yawning crevasses, outspread like lines of defence against any attempt to win the summit. Here every one of the party took off his shoes and drove stout steel caulks about half an inch long into them, having brought tools along for the purpose, and not having made use of them until now so that the points might not get dulled on the rocks ere the smooth, dangerous ice was reached. Besides being well shod each carried an alpenstock, and for special difficulties we had a hundred feet of rope and an axe.

Thus prepared, we stepped forth afresh, slowly groping our way through tangled lines of crevasses, crossing on snow-bridges here and there after cautiously testing them, jumping at narrow places, or crawling around the ends of the largest, bracing well at every point with our alpenstocks and setting our spiked shoes squarely down on the dangerous slopes. It was nerve-trying work, most of it, but we made good speed nevertheless, and by noon all stood together on the utmost summit, save one who, his strength failing for a time, came up later.

We remained on the summit nearly two hours, looking about us at the vast map-like views, comprehending hundreds of miles of the Cascade Range, with their black interminable forests and white volcanic cones in glorious array reaching far into Oregon; the Sound region also, and the great plains of eastern Washington, hazy and vague in the distance. Clouds began to gather. Soon of all the land only the summits of the mountains, St Helen's, Adams, and Hood, were left in sight, forming islands in the sky. We found two well-formed and well-preserved craters on the summit, lying close together like two plates on a table with their rims touching. The highest point of the mountain is located between the craters, where their edges come in contact. Sulphurous fumes and steam issue from several vents, giving out a sickening smell that can be detected at a considerable distance. The unwasted condition of these craters, and, indeed, to a great extent, of the entire mountain, would tend to show that Rainier is still a comparatively young mountain. With the exception of the projecting lips of the craters and the top of a subordinate summit a short distance to the northward, the mountain is solidly capped with ice all around; and it is this ice-cap which forms the grand central fountain whence all the twenty glaciers of Rainier flow, radiating in every direction.

The descent was accomplished without disaster, though several of the party had narrow escapes. One slipped and fell, and as he shot past me seemed to be going to certain death. So steep was the ice-slope no one could move to help him, but fortunately, keeping his presence of mind, he threw himself on his face and digging his alpenstock into the ice, gradually retarded his motion until he came to rest. Another broke through a slim bridge over a crevasse, but his momentum at the time carried him against the lower edge and only his alpenstock was lost in the abyss. Thus crippled by the loss of his staff, we had to lower him the rest of the way down the dome by means of the rope we carried. Falling rocks from the upper precipitous part of the ridge were also a source of danger, as they came whizzing past in successive volleys; but none told on us, and when we at length gained the gentle slopes of the lower ice-fields, we ran and slid at our ease, making fast, glad time, all care and danger past, and arrived at our beloved Cloud Camp before sundown.

We were rather weak from want of nourishment, and some suffered from sunburn, notwithstanding the partial protection of glasses and veils; otherwise, all were unscathed and well. The view we enjoyed from the summit could hardly be surpassed in sublimity and grandeur; but one feels far from home so high in the sky, so much so that one is inclined to guess that, apart from the acquisition of knowledge and the exhilaration of climbing, more pleasure is to be found at the foot of mountains than on their frozen tops. Doubly happy, however, is the man to whom lofty mountain-tops are within reach, for the lights that shine there illumine all that lies below.

14

JOHN MUIR'S ASCENT
OF MOUNT RAINER

Aubrey L Haines

from *Mountain Fever: Historic Conquests of Rainier.*

Not far to the south, a group of men were translating their memories of high places into something entirely new in the Pacific Northwest – an organisation of mountain climbers. And so on 7 October 1887, the Oregon Alpine Club came into existence at Portland.

That same year of 1887, John Muir received a proposal from the J Dewing Publishing Company, of San Francisco, to edit and contribute to an illustrated work to be called *Picturesque California.* Muir was then forty-nine years old, married and well settled upon his California ranch; but his heart was not there and his inspired writing had ceased.

Muir accepted the proposal and plunged with increasing enthusiasm into the new task, which brought him to Mount Rainier and accomplished much for both of them. His biographer says of his return to the wilderness world he loved so much: 'John Muir, in the fragmentary journals of these trips, resumed his writing. And he climbed Mount Rainier with something like the old ecstasy. "I didn't mean to climb it," he wrote to his wife, "but got excited and soon was on top".[1] Here was a man who had known the mountain fever before!

This should properly begin where John Muir boarded the Pullman car en route for the Pacific Northwest. He picked up his friend, the artist William Keith and wife, at Lake Tahoe, and together they continued slowly northward, collecting material as they went.[2]

On 20 July, 1888 they arrived at Seattle, where they were the guests of Attorney General J B Metcalfe, at whose home Mrs Keith was to stay during the Mount Rainier expedition. Several short excursions were made while the preparations for a mountain trip were completed; then some of those 'ambitious Seattle climbers' we have already met were found to accompany Muir.

One member of the Seattle group was Arthur Churchill Warner, a young photographer. Shortly after his return from the expedition he wrote to his father, describing the trip in a folksy, carelessly composed letter that has fortunately been preserved. He had this to say about the start:

> I was already to go to Alaska when a man came to me and said, 'We want you to go to Mount Rainier with us as special artist.' At first I said I could not go as I had to go to Alaska but when they said I must go and that I would be well paid I said 'All right' and on the morning of 8 August at three o'clock my alarm went off. I turned over, rubbed my eyes and got up, I had everything ready and was soon on the way to the train.
>
> Mr Ingraham went with me instead of going to Alaska. We had taken our traps down the night before and now we had a few small things to take. At the train we met the rest of the party, Mr John Muir, a well-known writer and explorer on the Coast. It was he who wanted me . . . William Keith an artist of California, D W Gass, Charles Piper, N O Booth, N Loomis, one of the compilers of the Loomis text books, used in the colleges east, E S Ingraham and Yours Truly. We were all on time, save Booth who was late and got left. The train went to Tacoma, then twenty miles to Yelm, where we got off and found we could not get our pack train until the next day, so we put up our tent, spent the day in making negatives, sketches, etc. Mr Bass and myself slept in a barn that night on new hay, the others in the tent and around the old rail fence. There are only two houses there and so we did not get beds.[3]

John Muir had an introduction to P B Van Trump, from their mutual friend, George B Bayley. He wanted the services of that veteran of two memorable ascents (who was then the storekeeper and postmaster at Yelm), as guide for the party. Muir calls him 'a volunteer', but the matter was not arranged that easily. Van Trump says, 'though my business and my wife being without help really made it a dereliction of duty for me to leave home, they soon talked me into the "mountain fever".'[4] Arrangements were also made with James Longmire to furnish pack and saddle animals, and two men to handle them.

They were at breakfast on the morning of the ninth when a freight train rattled by and Booth jumped off, completing the party. The pack train came up at 9.30, so the work of packing that 'cumbersome abundance of camp-stools and blankets' on the seven tough little cayuse ponies could begin.[5] The first animal loaded took off stiff-legged, quickly scattering the pack and making more work for the packers.

Of the two men furnished by Longmire, John Hays passed without comment, and remains nearly unknown;[6] but the other, Joe Stampfler, was an obvious youngster. Muir was concerned over the animals and the 'mere boy' who was to handle them, but he was told the ponies could stand up to their loads, and that Joe, though only fifteen years old, knew the diamond hitch and had managed pack strings before.[7] Joe's home was in Olympia, but he did not get along with his father, preferring to live with James Longmire's family, where he took care of the horses and did chores for his keep. He later became a well-known guide at Mount Rainier, yet Muir may have seen in him as he called him 'small queer Joe', the shadow of that persecution complex which finally led to self-destruction in the Tacoma waterway.

The expedition was on the road before eleven o'clock with Muir mounted on a horse called Bob Caribou, Keith on Dexter, a veteran of 1883 and Joe on an unnamed animal which was merely described as 'bones'. The remainder of the party followed afoot, leading the other animals with their 'huge, savage packs', which reminded Muir of a gypsy outfit. Muir's description of the Nisqually River crossing indicates the route followed was essentially that of 1870, though it is probable that rough wagon roads had replaced the trail for part of the way. Ten miles out they were joined by Van Trump, who came well mounted on a black pony, and evening found them eighteen miles from Yelm, at Indian Henry's farm, where all found beds in the barn. Muir described his host as 'a mild-looking, smallish man with three wives, three fields, and horses, oats, wheat and vegetables'. It was there at Mashel Prairie that they were afflicted with that sickness which followed them all the way to the mountain, causing them to question the freshness of their canned goods. However, Keith, the only one to escape the malady, says it was caused by rancid butter.[8]

Indisposed or not they were up at 4.30 on 10th August and soon passing through what Muir called 'glorious woods' on a trail as well defended by yellow-jackets as ever it had been. An encampment was made that evening at 'Forked Creek', a stream which can no longer be identified. They were on the way again at eight o'clock the following morning, reaching Kernahan's place in Succotash Valley at noon. Warner found the rancher to be a man he had formerly known in Omaha. Perhaps it was the Palisade Ranch Muir was thinking of when he wrote: 'The newcomers, building their cabins where the beavers once built theirs, keep a few cows and industriously seek to enlarge their small meadow patches by chopping, girdling and burning the edge of the encircling forest, gnawing like beavers, and scratching for a living among the blackened stumps and logs, regarding the trees as their greatest enemies – a sort of larger pernicious weed immensely difficult to get rid of.'

That night they arrived at Longmire's Springs (Soda Springs to some), where the development was yet rudimentary. A few feet north of the soda springs there was a log cabin about fifteen feet square, with a kitchen shed of cedar slabs, a shake roof and the stick-and-clay chimney so common on the frontier. A bathhouse of cedar slabs stood in the meadow west of the cabin, and the gentle rise behind it had been cleared to allow construction of a hotel, for which the wall frames had already been raised. James Longmire highly recommended the mineral waters to Muir: 'Drink at these springs and they will do you good. Every one's got medicine in them – a doctor said so – no matter what ails you.'

It appears those ailing travellers took the advice! It is likely they also listened with interest to the old pioneer's recital of his recent attempt to guide three men to the summit, which was his first and last experience in the guide business.[9]

On the morning of the 12th, 'all who had come through the ordeal of yellow-jackets, ancient meats and medicinal waters with sufficient strength', continued to their destination above Paradise Valley. The trail followed the west side of the Nisqually River to a point about one-half mile above the stream now known as Van Trump Creek, crossed the river, and climbed the ridge on the east side by switch-backs, reaching the top at the shallow notch called Canyon Rim. As the packhorses were plodding up that steep climb from the river, one of them was attacked by yellow-jackets. He was loaded with kitchen utensils and photographic equipment, and his bucking sent the tinware flying with a jangling that frightened other horses in the string. Stampfler says: 'Poor Warner was behind. He saw the stuff flying, and began dancing around like a wild man yelling, "Stop him; Oh, my plates! my plates"!' That put the rest of us to laughing and someone yelled back to him,

'To hell with your plates; it won't hurt them.'

We supposed he was worried about the tin plates, but he meant his photographic plates which he had carried so carefully all the way from Seattle.'[10] Fortunately, none were broken.

From the top of the switchbacks, the trail passed to the east of the prominent rocky knobs reaching a park-like forest at about 5000 feet above sea-level. Muir observed that 'Everyone of these parks, great and small, is a garden filled knee-deep with fresh, lovely flowers of every hue, the most luxuriant and the most extravagantly beautiful of all the alpine gardens I ever beheld in all my mountain-top wander-ings.' He had found his 'lower gardens of Eden'.

At two o'clock they found a campsite on the east shoulder of the little hill now known as Alta Vista. There, at Camp of the Clouds,[11] at the highest elevation at which horse feed and camp wood were available, the blankets were spread and the kettle was set to boiling, while the weary tourists lounged, sketched, and explored. Muir caught the beauty of that encampment in perfect prose: 'Out of the forest at last there stood the mountain, wholly unveiled, awful in bulk and majesty, filling all the view like a separate, new-born world, yet withal so fine and so beautiful it might well fire the dullest observer to desperate enthusiasm. Long we gazed in silent admira-tion, buried in tall daisies and anemones by the side of a snowbank.'

Warner, the photographer, at once climbed the little hill above the encampment and was entranced by what he saw. He was a vigorous, enthusiastic young man of twenty-four. Originally from Granby, Massachusetts, he came to the Puget Sound country in 1886 as a photographer for Henry Villard's Northern Pacific Railroad. Establishing himself in Seattle, he appears to have been well recommended when Muir needed an energetic cameraman. He was no naturalist, not even an outdoorsman, but he could see the untrammelled beauty around him. 'I looked back and saw such a view as I had newer seen before. Oh, if I had the power to describe it. At my feet was a bed of flowers such as I never thought could bloom . . . all was fresh, so new, so clean. The grass was short, fresh and green. There were not any old tin cans, newspapers . . . I never saw a city park so clean and so nice as that.' There you have a townsman's appreciative view!

That night Mount Rainier stood out in the bright moonlight in such ephemeral beauty that even weary travellers found it hard to go to sleep. The next morning was filled with botanising, sketching, picture-taking and preparation for an ascent of the mountain.

At two o'clock the climbing party, which did not include Keith or Joe Stampfler, left camp, all with light packs except Warner who had decided to take his camera.[12] A steady climb of five-and-a-half hours over steep snow-fields brought them to the foot of the rocky ridge now known as the Cowlitz Cleaver. There, on the saddle between the snow-field they had ascended and the Cowlitz Glacier, Muir saw light pumice sand, indicating a relatively sheltered spot. He recommended that they camp there at an elevation of 10,100 feet,[13] instead of going higher as Van Trump wished to do. Most of the party were suffering severely from fatigue and nausea and they readily agreed to a halt.

The work of making themselves comfortable for the night was begun at once. Ingraham says: 'Two by two we go to work preparing our beds. This we do by clearing away the loose stones from a space about three by six feet, stirring the sand with our pikes and making a wall of rocks around the cleared place. After a half hour's toil we declare our beds prepared. Hastily partaking of a little chocolate and hardtack, we "turned in", although the hour is early.'[14] One of the party was so sick he lay down apart from the others without making any attempt to protect himself from the cold, and might have suffered exposure if his comrades had not looked after him.

Daniel Waldo Bass, later an associate manager of the Frye Hotel in Seattle, probably did not think much of his accommodations that night. The single blanket brought for bedding failed to keep out the sharp northeast wind which blew hard enough to shower them with pumice sand all night; but, not being the kind to suffer in silence, he and Warner created a night-long diversion with wisecracks and buffoonery. Regardless it was a miserable night in which everyone's sleep was 'short and shallow', according to Muir.

In the grey dawn of the morning, those who could wolfed down a little breakfast before the party set off up the mountain, leaving their blankets behind at 'Camp Muir' as Ingraham called it.

They followed the rocky cleaver upward, occasionally descending onto the ice of Cowlitz Glacier to pass an obstruction. At the narrow ledge on the face of the great rock which Ingraham would later name 'Gibraltar' because of its similarity to the guardian of the Mediterranean, John Hays gave up the ascent and turned back. The snow in the chute was hummocky and gave them good footing, so they were soon up that treacherous groove. At 10.30 a.m. a stop was made at the 12,000 foot elevation to fit caulks into their shoes (half-inch steel caulks and tools to set them had been brought along). At that point, Warner cut his pants off at the knees so he could climb better, depending on a pair of long stockings for warmth. On the dome there was smooth, hard ice which required great caution in travelling, for a slip would certainly send the unfortunate climber sliding down into one of the many crevasses with which the steep slope was laced. Though a rope was brought, it was not used in the ascent; on dangerous slopes, they had no security other than careful placing of the feet and the support of the alpenstock each one carried. The smaller crevasses were vaulted but the necessity of crossing the larger ones on snow-bridges made the route devious.

Ingraham stayed ahead of the others in the ascent, giving Van Trump the impression he was impatient of guidance and expected to be the only one to reach the summit. Nor did he show any sympathy for the slow members of the party, as Muir did. Piper became exhausted toward the last, and Van Trump 'was much pleased by Muir's kindly sympathy for the lad, and with his cheering and encouraging words as he urged the wearied climber to push on to the goal, he meanwhile waiting for him.'[15]

The first climber reached the top at 11.45 a.m. on 14th August, 1888, while the plucky laggard made it an hour later. Without waiting to rest, Warner set up his camera, pulled off his coat to use as a focusing cloth, and proceeded to take the first photographs ever made on the summit of Mount Rainier. He nearly froze his unprotected arms getting those six views (two of groups of climbers atop the icy knob that forms the highest point, one at each crater, one toward the North Peak and one toward the south peak). Warner's negatives were unusual for another reason; some of them were made on sheet film, the first ever used in the Pacific Northwest. He had received a few pieces in the mail just before going to the mountain and took them along for use in case he broke his sensitised glass plates.

Less than two hours were spent on the summit. Van Trump managed to get one of the party to go with him to look at the nearly filled-in hole where he, Bayley, and Longmire spent such a miserable night in 1883. But when it came to continuing on to the North Peak (Liberty Cap) with him, none would go.

While they were on the mountain-top clouds began to form below them, interrupting the grand view and creating the fear that a storm was brewing, so all but Van Trump were anxious to be off the summit. Briefly he stood there, debating with 'the spirit of precaution, reinforced by thoughts of the wife and the little ones' whether to remain and attempt the North Peak alone, or descend with his companions; but he bowed to Muir's opinion of the weather situation, and, with a 'longing, lingering look' at the unexplored peak, he turned to follow the others down.

As is often the case, the descent was more perilous than the wearying upward struggle. One of the snow-bridges crossed came near to ending the career of Charles Vancouver Piper. Most of the party had crossed ahead of the twenty-one-year-old botanist, but instead of walking over, he placed his alpenstock near the middle and vaulted across. Though he landed safely on the other side, the bridge collapsed, carrying his staff down with it. The others offered to lower Piper into the crevasse on a rope to recover his alpenstock but he declined – and lived to become a noted agristologist of the United States Department of Agriculture.[16]

Van Trump was immediately behind Piper, for he had been the last to leave the summit, and loss of the snow-bridge forced him to vault over deliberately. He managed it, landing 'somewhat astride of the homeward side of the crevasse'. Muir indicates there was a third mishap when one of the party slipped and fell. He says: 'So steep was the ice-slope no one could move to help him, but fortunately, keeping his presence of mind, he threw himself on his face and digging his alpenstock into the ice, gradually retarded his motion until he came to rest.'

Piper was assisted down the icy portion of the dome with the rope, though the manner in which it was done sounds unsafe in the light of present rope technique. One of the climbers would go down a reasonable distance, set his alpenstock firmly and attach one end of the rope to it with a half-hitch; then Piper would take the other end and walk down past the anchorage as far as the rope would go. However, he did get down safely.

Gibraltar Rock was reached at 3.30 p.m. which assured them a dangerous passage of the ledge, under a bombardment of rocks and ice loosened from the cliff above by the warmth of the sun. Ingraham was narrowly missed by a shower of boulders he described as 'singing as merrily as a cannon ball just shot from a thirty-pounder'. A different ledge (narrower but less exposed than the one crossed when ascending) was used, yet it was a harrowing experience.

The remainder of the descent was easily accomplished. Below Camp Muir some were able to slide quickly down by means of a standing glissade, balancing with the alpenstock, and the last straggler reached Camp of the Clouds by seven o'clock.

The members of the summit party were easily identified the next day. In addition to the weakness resulting from insufficient nourishment while under great physical strain, there were bruises, sunburned hands and faces, and weakened eyes. Dan Bass was quite sick and so snow-blind he had to be led about the camp, while Warner's sunburned lips became a raw sore.

A warmer campsite was soon found at a lower elevation; then Muir made what are probably the earliest measurements of the rate of flow of the Nisqually Glacier. By setting stakes he found it moved twelve inches in twenty-two hours. On the 16th, the party began to break up. Van Trump and Dan Bass left for Yelm, while Ingraham, Piper, and Booth passed around the east side of the mountain, across the Cowlitz and White River glaciers to the Bailey Willis trail, which they followed to Wilkeson.[17]

On the 18th, the camp equipment was packed and moved to Longmire's Springs, where Muir, Keith, and Warner rested over Sunday. That would appear to be the day Warner took that earliest photograph of James Longmire's development there. The plan had been to start homeward on Monday, but the horses prevented it by returning to the lush meadows at Camp of the Clouds; they had to be tracked and brought back, which consumed the entire day.

A start was finally made at 8.30 on 21st August, but trouble with the packs prevented them from getting farther than Kernahan's farm that day. There they were able to get a good meal and a bed in the barn. They reached Indian Henry's farm the next night, enjoying the comfort of his barn for a second time, then pushed on to Yelm, where they arrived in mid-afternoon. At Van Trump's house they had what Warner called 'the first good meal we had eaten for two weeks'.

So ended a notable expedition to Mount Rainier. From it would come the first description of the mountain and its beautiful alpine parks to reach the American people generally. Though both Kautz and Stevens wrote accounts in the year 1876, theirs were both too early and too much concerned merely with mountain climbing to do much for the mountain. In contrast, John Muir was a popular writer, writing at an opportune time, for the United States Coast Survey had just released the results of the 1870 measurement of Mount Rainier's height by angulation from the west.[18] On the basis of a computed elevation of 14,444 feet, it was thought to be the highest mountain in the United States, which explains the intense interest with which Muir's words were read.

NOTES AND REFERENCES

1. Linnie Marsh Wolfe (ed.) *John of the Mountains* (Boston 1938), p.282.
2. Brother Cornelius, *Keith, Old Master of California* (New York, c.1942), p.167.
3. Aubrey L Haines (ed.), 'John Muir's Ascent of Mount Rainier as Recorded by his Photographer, AC Warner' in *The Mountaineer* December 1956, pp.38–45. This account is used frequently hereafter without citation.

4. PB Van Trump, letter to George B Bayley, 26th August 1888 (published in *Oakland Tribune*, 23rd July to 13th August 1939). This account is used frequently hereafter without citation.

5. John Muir (ed.), *Picturesque California, the Rocky Mountains and the Pacific Slope* (New York, 1888), pp.286–88. This account used frequently hereafter without citation.

6. John Hays helped build the 'homestead cabin' at Longmire Spring in 1889. See 'Narrative of James Longmire: A Pioneer of 1853', in *WHQ*, xxiii: pp.47–56, 138–50.

7. Fourteen years old according to ES Ingraham's 'Then and Now' in *The Mountaineer*, December 1915, p.56.

8. Brother Cornelius, op. cit.

9. *Tacomian*, 21st January, 1843: 'Personal. Allen C Mason, Frank Ross and FS Harmon, climbed the mountain to a height of 13,050 ft. during the week ending June 22, 1888, with James Longmire as guide.'.

10. Joseph Stampfler, 'Climbing Mount Tacoma', in *Tacoma News*, 12th July 1907.

11. The original Camp of the Clouds was at an elevation of 5700ft and should not be confused with the tent-camp of the same name established later on the south side of Alta Vista (elevation 5530ft).

12. Warner had a large view camera which was crude by present standards. It was eighteen inches long with a body twelve inches square; the lens had a speed of f.22 and lacked a shutter. Exposures were made by plucking a black cap from the lens and replacing it after the exposure was made. The camera, with its tripod, glass plates and other items weighed over fifty pounds.

13. Muir was carrying his favourite aneroid barometer which gave him a reading of 10,000 feet.

14. ES Ingraham, 'Discovery of Camp Muir', in Meany's *Mount Rainier*, pp.150–58. Reprinted from the *Puget Sound Magazine*, published in Seattle. The magazine probably perished with the Seattle Fire, for no file of it is known to exist, though the faculty records of the University of Washington refer to it.

15. In his brief article, 'On Top of Tacoma', in *Tacoma Ledger*, 19 August, 1888, Van Trump gives the impression Warner brought up the rear, but other accounts establish that it was Piper.

16. Piper graduated from the University of Washington in 1885 and became a professor of botany and zoology at Washington Agricultural College, 1892–1903. His version of the 'near-accident' was given in 'A Narrow Escape' in *The Mountaineer*, VIII (December 1915), pp.52–53.

17. Ingraham indicates that Norman Booth died prior to February 1893, see 'Mr. Ingraham's Letter' in *Tacomian* 4th February 1893.

18. The measurement was made by James Smyth Lawson, member of a Coast Survey Party under Prof. GC Davidson, from a base-line near Puget Sound. See 'It Rises Above All' in *Seattle Post Intelligencer*, 12th August, 1894.

BIBLIOGRAPHY

BOOKS AND EDITED COLLECTIONS OF JOHN MUIR'S WRITINGS:
The Mountains of California, John Muir (Century, New York 1894)
Our National Parks, John Muir (Houghton Mifflin & Co., Boston, 1901)
My First Summer in the Sierra, John Muir (Houghton Mifflin, Boston 1911)
The Yosemite, John Muir (Century, New York 1912)
The Story of My Boyhood and Youth, John Muir (Houghton Mifflin, Boston 1913)
Travels in Alaska, John Muir, edited by William Frederic Badè (Houghton Mifflin, Boston 1915)
A Thousand Mile Walk to the Gulf, John Muir (Houghton Mifflin, Boston 1916)
The Cruise of the Corwin, John Muir, edited by William Frederic Badè (Houghton Mifflin, Boston 1917)
Steep Trails, John Muir, ed. by William Frederic Badè (Houghton Mifflin, Boston 1918)
Stickeen, John Muir (1909; Houghton Mifflin, Boston 1923)
John Muir, To Yosemite and Beyond: Writings from the Years 1863 to 1875, edited by Robert Engberg and Donald Wesling (Madison, University of Wisconsin Press, 1980)
John Muir, Summering in the Sierra, edited by Robert Engberg (University of Wisconsin 1984)
John Muir in His Own Words – A book of Quotations, compiled and edited by Peter Browning (Great West Books, Lafayette, California 1988)
The Eight Wilderness-Discovery Books, edited by Terry Gifford (Diadem, London 1992)
The Wilderness Journeys (The Story of My Boyhood & Youth, The Thousand Mile Walk to the Gulf, My First Summer in the Sierra, Travels in Alaska and Stickeen), edited and introduced by Graham White, (Canongate Books, Edinburgh 1996)
John Muir, Mountaineering Essays, edited and introduced by Richard Fleck (University of Utah Press 1997)

BIOGRAPHIES AND OTHER BOOKS:
The Life and Letters of John Muir, edited by William Frederic Badè (2 vols, Houghton Mifflin, Boston 1924) republished as *John Muir, His Life and Letters & Other Writings,* edited by Terry Gifford (Baton-Wicks Publishing, 1996)
John of the Mountains: The Unpublished Journals of John Muir, edited by Linnie Marsh Wolfe (1938: University of Wisconsin Press, 1979)

Sacred Summits

Son of the Wilderness, The Life of John Muir by Linnie Marsh Wolfe (University of
Wisconsin Press, 1945, 1973)
John Muir and His Legacy: The American Conservation Movement by Stephen Fox
(Boston: Little, Brown & Co., 1981)
The Pathless Way: John Muir and the American Wilderness by Michael P. Cohen
(University of Wisconsin Press, 1984)
Baptized into Wilderness, A Christian Perspective on John Muir, by Richard Cartwright
Austin (Creekside Press, Abingdon, Virginia, 1991)
John Muir, Life and Work, edited by Sally Miller (University of New Mexico Press
1993)
John Muir, His Life and Letters & Other Writings, edited and introduced by Terry
Gifford (Baton-Wicks Publishing, 1996)
John Muir, From Scotland to the Sierra, a biography by Frederick Turner (Canongate
Books, Edinburgh, 1998)
Alaska Days with John Muir, Samuel Hall Young (New York, FH Revell Co. 1915)

OTHER BOOKS REFERRED TO:
Highland Landscape – A Survey by WH Murray, (Commissioned by the National
Trust for Scotland, Aberdeen University Press 1962)
Percy Unna – The Man Who Bought Mountains by Rennie McOwan, (National Trust
for Scotland brochure)
History of the Sierra Nevada by Francis P Farquhar (Berkely, University of California
Press, 1966)
Mountain Fever, Historic Conquests of Rainier by Aubrey L Haines (Oregon
Historical Society 1962)
The Climber's Guide to the High Sierra by Steve Roper (Sierra Club Books, San
Francisco, 1976)
Walden by Henry David Thoreau (Boston, Ticknor and Fields 1862)

The Wilderness Journeys

John Muir

Introduced by Graham White

'A remarkable, self-effacing but brilliant man, an adventurer and naturalist, whose work paved the way for America's expansive national park system . . . Truly the stuff that heroes are made of.'

Steve Lawson

The name of John Muir has come to stand for the protection of wild land and wilderness in both America and Britain. Born in Dunbar in 1838, Muir is famed as the father of American conservation. This collection, including the rarely seen *Stickeen*, presents the finest of Muir's travel writings, and imparts a rounded portrait of a man whose generosity, passion, discipline and vision are an inspiration to this day.

Combining acute observation with a sense of inner discovery, Muir's writings of his travels through some of the greater landscapes on Earth, including the Carolinas, Florida, Alaska and those lands which were to become the great National Parks of Yosemite and the Sierra Valley, raise an awareness of nature to a spiritual dimension. These journals provide a unique marriage of natural history with lyrical prose and often amusing anecdotes, retaining a freshness, intensity and brutal honesty which will amaze the modern reader.

Includes: *The story of My Boyhood and Youth, A Thousand Mile Walk to the Gulf, My First Summer in the Sierra, Stickeen* and *Travels in Alaska.*

(Canongate Classic) 640 pages £9.99 pbk (UK) ISBN 0 86241 586 1 $15.95 (US)

Kingdoms of Experience

EVEREST, THE UNCLIMBED RIDGE

Andrew Greig

Introduced by Chris Bonington

'a wonderful, gritty expedition book' Chris Bonington

'a classic in mountaineering literature' *Geographical Magazine*

In March 1985, Mal Duff led a new expedition to conquer Everest by the unclimbed north-east ridge. The last attempt by a Chris Bonington team had ended in failure and the tragic deaths of two great climbers, Joe Tasker and Pete Boardman.

Everyone knew the risks as well as the excitement of the challenge. In this extraordinary book, shortlisted for the Boardman-Tasker Awards, Greig chronicles not only the assault on the peak but also the complex inter-relationships of nineteen very different individuals living together, yet each of them very much alone.

Andrew Greig is regarded as one of the leading poets of his generation and as a popular literary novelist. His previous climbing book, *Summit Fever*, also published by Canongate, was described as 'one of the best expedition books so far . . . an excellent read.' (*The Climber*).

288 pages, colour plate section £9.99 pbk (UK) ISBN 0 86241 881 X $15 (US)